The Coach Business Guide: The Path to Launch and Grow Your Coaching Practice

Rhonda Boyle and Anne Herbster

Copyright © 2022 C&C Business Strategies, LLC

Copyright

All rights reserved. No part of this book shall be reproduced, stored in a retrieval system, or transmitted by any means, electronic, mechanical, photocopying, recording or otherwise, without written permission from the authors. Except in the case of brief quotations embodied in critical reviews © and certain other noncommercial uses permitted by copyright law. For permission send requests by email to CandCbusinessstrategies@gmail.com

Limit of Liability/Disclaimer of Warranty:

The authors have used their best efforts in preparing this book, they make no representations or warranties with respect to the accuracy or completeness of the contents in this book. The book is sold with the understanding that the authors are not engaged in rendering legal, tax, accounting, or other professional services. The advice and strategies contained in the book may not be suitable for every situation. This book is not intended to replace the professional counsel of experts (legal, accounting, marketing, etc.) in these matters. The authors shall not be liable for any loss of profit or any other commercial damages including, but not limited to special, incidental, consequential, or other damages.

Although every precaution has been taken in the preparation of this book, the authors assume no responsibility for errors and omissions. Neither is any liability assumed for damages resulting from the use of information contained herein.

ISBN: 9780578362168

Cover Designer: Margaret Herbster

Book Layout and Design: Mariah St. Jeor

Copyeditor: Lisa Herbster

Published By: C&C Business Strategies Publishing

Testimonials

"I wish I had this book when I started! I have used all these strategies; however, they have been pieced together from resources I had to search for. These pages were invaluable in getting to the most important: who you serve, what they need, and how you will make change happen. This book can be a comprehensive one-stop for the basics of getting the business started with a call to find someone to help you get there."

 - Yolanda Gray
Certified Holistic Life Coach

"Many professional coaches pursue certifications in preparation for offering their services. Essential when planning for or launching a coaching business is preparing the foundation for that business. Most certification programs do not provide this vital information. Rhonda and Anne provide much needed guidance in all aspects of establishing a fulfilling and lucrative coaching business. They cover all the bases, sharing their knowledge and providing valuable exercises that move you forward. No coach desiring success should be without this valuable resource!"

 - Joann O'Neil
Strengths Activation Coach

"Cover to cover, lesson to lesson, exercise to exercise this is a dynamic set of information too important to miss. If you are serious about coaching and helping others, this is your guide to success."

 - Mark Greeley
Independent Consultant

"Coaches are in the unique position of being both coach and entrepreneur. Most are not prepared for the latter. The Coach Business Guide provides the way for a coach to put the fundamentals of running their own business success - specifically the who, what and why."

 - Clint Carlos
Co-Founder and CEO of Soar.com

"I highly recommend The Coach Business Guide to any coach starting a business or who needs to invigorate their current business. Not only is this book packed with fundamental and mind-expanding information, but the exercises are invaluable.

- Michelle Gunn
Gallup Certified Strengths Coach at Cultivate and Thrive

"The Coach Business Guide provided much needed guidance and accountability in establishing my area of focus. The book was invaluable with respect to creating a well thought out business, marketing, social media, and life balance plan. I found invaluable clarity as I engaged in the step-by-step exercises. Without this material, I would still be lacking critical components necessary to grow a flourishing and fulfilling speaking and coaching practice."

- Buddy Estrella
Aspiring Identity Coach & Speaker

"If you feel called to be a coach, it's probably because you care about people and want to use your amazing talents to help others overcome challenges and experience success. I admire coaches. You change lives! You transform organizations! You can do so much good! But coaching is not only a calling--it's a profession. It requires clients. That takes way more business, sales, and marketing processes to be set up than most people-oriented-people want to believe. **That's why you need this amazing book!** Rhonda and Anne have created a step-by-step roadmap that you can follow. As you follow their advice you'll find yourself coaching more and being busy with your business, less. I highly recommend this excellent resource."

- Paul Allen
Founder Ancestry.com CEO Soar.com (AI Marketplace)

Dedication

We dedicate this book to coaches everywhere who are committed to helping their clients in their transformational journey. Their unwavering support for the process of human development inspires us to continue our own focus of helping coaches build their successful practice.

> "Believe in what you want so much that it has no choice but to materialize."
> - Karen Salmanson

Acknowledgments:

Writing this book has been a labor of love and we could not have completed this without the input, support and help of so many. Special thanks to our core group of coaches who worked with us to review and provide feedback: Elizabeth Craig, Buddy Estrella, Sheena Fleener, Mark Greeley, Michelle Gunn, Debby Lissaur and Joann O'Neill. We also appreciate the artwork and design of Margaret Herbster and Mariah St. Jeor. And of course, special gratitude to our families, who were patient and supportive.

We cannot thank you enough!

Table of Contents

Identify   5
- Getting Started   7
  - Exercise - Support and Resources   11
- Defining Your Expertise   13
  - Exercise - Experiences   14
  - Exercise - Environmental Preference   14
  - Exercise - Training, Degrees, Certifications, and Intellectual Property   15
  - Exercise - Specialized Focus   15
- Your Calling, Your Vision, Your Beliefs   19
  - Exercise - Defining Your Calling   20
  - Exercise - What is Your Vision for Your Practice   21
  - Exercise - What Beliefs are Important to You?   22
- Getting Focused   25
  - Exercise - Defining Your Focus   26
- Identify Your Ideal Client   29
  - Exercise - Identify Your Corporate Clients   31
  - Exercise - Identify Your Individual Clients   32
- Identify How You Will Work   35
  - Exercise - Identify How You Will Work   41

Create   45
- Your Coaching Process   47
- Before and After Transformation   51
  - Exercise - Client Transformation Journey   52
  - Exercise - Personal Client Transformation   52
  - Exercise - Corporate Client Transformation   53
- Define Your Materials   57
  - Exercise - Define Your Materials   58
- Creating a Basic Workshop   61
  - Exercise - Workshop Basic Information   62

Exercise - Workshop Objectives and Outcomes	63
Exercise - Workshop Materials and Exercises	64
Exercise - Workshop Follow Up Planning	65
Exercise - Workshop Name	66
Exercise - Workshop Description	68
Mapping Out Your Workshop	71
Exercise - Mapping Out Your Workshop	75
Creating a One-to-One Coaching Package	79
Exercise - Package Basic Information	80
Exercise - Package Objectives and Outcomes	81
Exercise - Package Materials Needed	82
Exercise - Package Follow Up Planning	83
Exercise: Package Individual Session Focus	85
Exercise - Package Name	86
Exercise - Package Description	88
Exercise: Mapping Your One-to-One Package	90
Some Assembly Required	93
Pricing	97
Exercise - Pricing Your Coaching Package or Workshop	99
Plan	103
Planning for Your Financial Success	105
Work Week	109
Exercise - Time Available	110
Investment and Income Needs	113
Exercise - Investment and Income Needs	114
Exercise - Current Expenses	115
Exercise - Determining Your Income	118
Launch	121
Getting Ready to Launch	123
Package and Workshop Messaging	125
Exercise - Keyword Brainstorm	126

Exercise - Keyword Selections	127
Creating Your Key Messaging	129
Exercise - Opening Statement	131
Exercise - Challenging Questions	133
Exercise - Knowing the Consequences	135
Exercise - Giving Hope	136
Exercise - Working Together	138
Exercise - Call to Action	140
Exercise - Pulling it all Together	142
Getting Your Business Started	145
Exercise - Getting Paid	148
Getting Your First Clients	151
Exercise: Short Biography	156
Grow	**161**
Growing Your Business	163
Referrals and Testimonials	167
Exercise - Referrals and Testimonials	168
Networking	171
Exercise - Networking Opportunities	173
Exercise - What Do You Do?	175
Developing Your Brand	181
Exercise - Brand Imagery	182
Marketing Assets	185
Exercise - Promotional Assets and Needs	186
Developing Marketing Content	189
Exercise - Marketing Content	191
Social Media	193
Public Speaking and Events	197
Multiple Streams of Income	201
Tools for Continued Growth	205
Final Thoughts of the Book	**211**
About the Authors	**213**

Introduction

Have you ever thought, *"I love to help other people. How can I create a business that will allow me to work for myself while helping others?"* If you have, maybe now is the time to start your own business as a coach, consultant, or trainer. This book has been designed just for you! It will help you **identify, create, plan, launch,** and **grow** your coaching practice. It was designed for any coach - whether a life coach, business coach, wellness coach, or otherwise.

This book provides step-by-step guidance to start and launch your coaching business. Whether you are launching your coaching practice or you feel your business needs a refresh, we strongly encourage you to start at the beginning and go through each of the exercises sequentially. To be successful, you must schedule time on your calendar each week to go through the book and the exercises. We recommend that you block at least four hours a week to be sure you stay on track with your launch goals.

Where is the Coaching Industry Going?

Coaching has now been pushed mainstream. More and more companies and individuals are recognizing the value of coaching. In today's climate - with people changing jobs, re-education as a result of culture change, and technology advancements - people are turning to coaching in order to align their interests and needs with changing opportunities.

The Coaching industry is exploding. According to the 2020 International Coaching Federation (ICF) study[1], there are approximately 71,000 coaches worldwide with about a third of them residing in the United States. The market itself is estimated to be worth over $1 billion dollars. In the *Sherpa Executive Coaching Survey Summary 2020*[2], hourly coaching rates range

---

1 International Coaching Federation "2020 ICF Global Coaching Study" https://coachestrainingblog.com/becomeacoach/a-look-into-the-202-icfglobal-coaching-study
2 Sherpa Coaching "2020 Executive Coaching Survey summary" https://www.sherpacoaching.com/annualexecutive-coaching-survey/

from Life Coaches at $160 per hour to Executive Coaches earning $325 an hour. These rates are averages, and many coaches charge higher rates based on their experience and area of focus. Successful coaches, depending on their area of expertise, on average work with up to eleven clients at any given time.

Research suggests that Life and Executive Coaching will continue to grow. There may be some reduction due to environmental factors, but overall, companies are looking for coaching for their leaders, teams and employees. In addition, people are tired and want to do something new and different. Jobs are changing. Many are choosing to reinvent themselves in their later years instead of retiring. All of these dynamics provide opportunities for coaching.

We recognize that there is a lot of material here to work through. If you get stuck, be sure to reach out for help and additional resources at our website. You can find us at *www.CoachBusinessGuide.com.*

Let's get started!

Identify

One of the most courageous things you can do is identify yourself, know who you are, what you believe in and where you want to go.
- Sheila Murray Bethel, PhD

1
Getting Started

The world of coaching is expanding as more people look for help. There are many different areas that can be chosen as the focus of a coaching business. For example, you may have heard of the terms Relationship coach or Health & Wellness coach. Other options include, but are not limited to, Career coaching, Business coaching, C-Suite Executive or Team coaching. There are a wide variety of possibilities depending on your personal preferences and areas of expertise. If you are unsure of the type of coaching best suited to your specific skills, there are exercises in the next few chapters that will help you uncover your coaching focus.

Remember, a wonderful aspect of coaching is that it provides the freedom to create a niche based upon personal experience. For example, we have worked with a client who found herself navigating a health crisis. That experience led her to become a Care coach, helping others through crises with loved ones. That was not the direction she initially envisioned. Be open to considering all aspects of your abilities when trying to choose the coaching style best suited to you.

Throughout this book, there are exercises that include specific questions which will help guide you through the processes of launching and growing a coaching business. To get the most benefit from this book, we recommend you have a notebook or journal dedicated specifically to note-taking along this career journey. We strongly encourage you to thoughtfully answer the questions and write them in your journal. These answers will provide insights that will help you grow personally and professionally as you build your business.

At the top of the first page of your journal, write today's date and the date you wish to launch your coaching practice or refresh the focus of your existing business. It is important that you declare a date. Neglecting this detail will likely delay your success.

Things to Consider

Starting your own business is challenging. As you begin to look at a career as a coach or consultant, be aware that there are some pitfalls or misconceptions that may get in the way of your success. Recognizing them when they come up and having a strategy in place beforehand can mean you are always able to move forward.

We want to address isolation. Being a "lone ranger" can lead you down a path of missed opportunities, greater frustration, and ultimately, failure. You need the support of others - your family and friends and other experts. You will need mentorship and coaching for yourself, too. Do not let yourself become overwhelmed in this new endeavor. There is no need to do this alone. There will be other things to think about as you move forward. You might need the advice of a lawyer or an accountant, for example, to provide business advice and expertise.

Another aspect to remember is that starting any new business takes time. Launching a coaching practice is not a "get rich quick" scheme. If you have a job, now is not the time to quit!

Identify - Getting Started

You have a lot of work to do with your new startup, and you will likely need cash flow from your current position. It is unrealistic to think that you can "build it" and they will come. There is a process that works well to get your business up and running successfully. In the coming sections, we will provide guidance to help you **identify, create, plan, launch** and **grow** your coaching practice.

If you are in the early stages of creating your startup, think about additional training, education, certifications and/or material development that would assist you in building a successful business. These are likely investments you will want to make in order to position yourself in the marketplace.

Remember, you now want to be "the boss". It is crucial that you prepare and educate yourself to the best of your ability as you embark on this new endeavor. Always be open to learning something new. Always look for new ways to grow and expand your business. Be willing to put yourself in new situations that will allow you to meet people who will help you rise to where you want to grow. Finally, always expect change!

Challenges of Starting Your Coaching Business

As with any vocation or career, there are challenges to going out on your own.

Guess what coaches do best... they coach! Once you step outside of the realm of coaching, consulting, and serving your clients, there are numerous pitfalls that may lie in your path and cause problems for your business.

There are times when you may need to find outside experts to help you. We will cover these topics in depth later, but you should start thinking about these things now. Determine what skills and abilities you already possess and where you will need outside assistance for the following:

- Business Development
- Financial
- Marketing
- Networking
- Pricing and Packaging
- Program and Training Development
- Sales
- Social Media
- Technology

Your Support and Resources

Before you jump in and try to run a coaching business, we recommend you go through a series of exercises to help set the foundation. These exercises will help you get to the root of your desire, the time you have available to devote to your passion, and the people and resources you already have around you for support.

It is critical to identify your support system to help you stay focused on launching your coaching practice. By choosing people who will hold you accountable, you will have a far greater chance of staying on track and building the coaching business you want.

Find a quiet place. With the journal or notebook you have dedicated for writing along this journey, take time to complete the following exercise. These questions will help you determine what you are starting with and who is already part of your support system. You should already have declared your launch date and written it down.

Identify - Getting Started

Exercise - Support and Resources

Answer the following to identify your support team:

Who can you lean on for help and what support can they provide?

Which family members or friends will support you in your new endeavor?

Are there other coaches to whom you can reach out to for suggestions?

Do you have a business mentor who you can meet with regularly?

How many hours a week will you dedicate to starting your business?

What amount are you ready to invest in starting your business?

What will get in the way of you being able to spend time on your business, eg: family, work?

Review your responses and be honest with yourself. Do you have the support of your family and friends? Do you have mentors or peer coaches who can help answer questions or help you solve challenges? Are you ready to invest the time and energy it will take to launch your business successfully?

Support and resources are necessary to help you successfully move forward in launching your coaching practice.

2
Defining Your Expertise

Now the work begins! Time to make decisions about what kind of coaching you will be doing. Earlier, we shared some examples of different types of coaching. Take a moment to think and plan what your business will look like. Talk to friends, coworkers or people who you identified earlier to give you suggestions, ideas, and recommendations.

Personal and Professional Experiences

Your personal experiences are significant to who you are and they provide insight into your interests and expertise. You have also developed skills that can cross industries and enhance your coaching style.

The following exercises will help you identify what skills, credentials and experience you have that can be used to create and define your business. Included are questions concerning what training materials and exercises you have access to or have created. There are also questions regarding your environmental preference and your specialized focus. Having clarity about these areas will help you choose a direction and a focus in the coming chapters. Use your journal to document your answers.

The Coach Business Guide

Exercise - Experiences

Answer the following to identify your experiences and skills that can be utilized in your coaching practice.

What do you have a lot of experience in?

In what industries do you have familiarity and knowledge?

Where have you worked?

What unique skills do you have that are valued by certain industries?

Exercise - Environmental Preference

Answer the following to identify how you want to work.

How would you like to work with clients:

   In a One-to-One setting?

   In a One-to-Many setting?

Would you like to work in a virtual setting or live and in person?

Identify - Defining Your Expertise

Exercise - Training, Degrees, Certifications, and Intellectual Property

Answer the following to describe what materials and training you have access to and what you are authorized to facilitate.

Training and Coaching Resources

Do you have any unique training?

What tools and resources do you have access to?

What programs are you certified to lead?

Advanced Degrees or Certifications

Do you have special academic degrees that are relevant to your practice?

What coaching or business certifications do you have?

Intellectual Property

What original workshops have you created?

What worksheets, forms or surveys have you designed?

Exercise - Specialized Focus

Provide information about any unique industries, interests or relationships you have.

In what area or industry are you interested in working?

Do you have existing relationships that provide a built-in network?

The Coach Business Guide

Based on your exploration, do you recognize that you already have skills, experiences and expertise that can be used in your coaching business? Does this give you the confidence to know that you are capable of this? You are not starting from scratch. If you have gaps in your expertise, do not worry about it. There will be plenty of opportunities to add to your education along the way.

3

Your Calling, Your Vision, Your Beliefs

Since you have identified the skills and expertise that you have to support your coaching business, let's make sure that your decision is in alignment with your personal calling, your vision and your beliefs.

This is a critical step in defining your practice and exploring what is important to you and will guide you as you move forward. Use your journal to record your answers to the following exercises.

Your Personal Calling

Most coaches feel a sense of "calling" to coach. They cannot NOT coach. It's just part of who they are and what they instinctively do. Getting clear on what is calling you to coach and start a practice will benefit you. Not only will you be happier and fulfilled, you will find excitement and joy in your life!

The Coach Business Guide

The following exercise will bring clarity on what calls you to coach.

Exercise - Defining Your Calling

Answer the following to help you determine why you are called to coach.

Why are you a coach or trainer?

What calls you to coach for a living?

What motivates you to start your own coaching practice?

What difference do you want to make in the world around you?

Your Vision

Seeing your coaching business in your imagination can help drive you towards your vision and goals. We have all heard that if you do not know where you are going, you will never get there. We suggest that if you do not SEE where you are going, it will be difficult to get there. Roadmaps are great. Check lists are helpful. At the end of the day, your inner vision can be the most powerful guide to make your dreams of a coaching business come true.

The next exercise will allow you to explore what you see for your coaching business. Spend time here journaling or perhaps even meditating, until you know what you want.

Identify - Your Calling, Your Vision, Your Beliefs

> **Exercise - What is Your Vision for Your Practice**
> Answer the following questions to
> determine the direction you would like
> your business to take in the future.
>
> *Imagine your coaching practice in the future. What do you see yourself doing?*
>
> *What are some of the goals you want to accomplish?*
>
> *Where do you see your business one year from now?*
>
> *Looking forward five years from now, where do you see your practice going?*

Your Beliefs

Your personal beliefs will drive decision making in your practice. These beliefs will keep you in alignment if you understand what they are. Knowing your boundaries and values will alert you when presented with something that is contrary to what you believe in. This will empower you to say NO when necessary and make better decisions around the business you pursue.

In the next exercise, you will examine some of the beliefs you hold dear.

> ### Exercise - What Beliefs are Important to You?
> Answer the following questions to better understand the beliefs that drive you.
>
> *Name five things that are important to you that are unchanging?*
>
> *What behaviors do you value the most?*
>
> *Are there guiding principles that you live by in your day-to-day life?*
>
> *What are your personal boundaries? What is not okay with you?*
>
> *How will your coaching practice have a positive impact on the beliefs you hold dear?*
>
> *How will the work you do align with these beliefs?*

There are many things to think through as you look over your responses to these questions. Do you understand your boundaries and limits? Do you see what is most meaningful to you in your life? Will you be able to carry that into your coaching practice?

Now is the time to make sure there is alignment between where you are currently in your life, where you envision yourself in the future, who you are as a person, and what kind of business you believe you will enjoy.

4

Getting Focused

Next in the process of getting started on your journey to running your own business, you will need to choose and define the focus of your coaching practice. This will likely change over time as you identify new areas of interest for yourself. At this point, you should have a general idea of what you bring to the table and why you want to be a coach.

Lack of Focus

You love coaching, and therefore, it's intuitive to want to coach anyone and everyone, regardless of their challenges. Unfortunately, an unfocused practice is at higher risk of failure. By not narrowing your target market, you run the risk of being fragmented and having too many areas of interest. This can lead to an inability to create clear messaging that your ideal client can hear.

The Coach Business Guide

In your journal, write down who you want to serve and why. Give this time and thought.

Exercise - Defining Your Focus

Looking back, use the information from previous exercises to answer the following questions and gain clarity on your focus.

Who do you want to serve?

What do you care about?

What do you want to change in the world?

What do people come to you for already?

What do you want to focus on in your coaching business?

Looking over your responses to these questions, do you feel excited about the area(s) you have chosen to focus your coaching business on? Do you feel enthusiastic about who you will serve and the opportunities that lie ahead? If you answered "no," then you have additional work to do in this section. Share the exercises you have completed so far with your mentor and your support group and seek their input.

What you choose now will be the foundation for the rest of the book, so make sure you are ready to commit. Even if you do not have your focus defined completely, pick something with which to work through the remaining exercises. You can always change your focus later!

5
Identify Your Ideal Client

Remember, as you set up your coaching practice there is a lot more to creating a new business than just putting out your shingle and expecting clients to arrive on your doorstep. A clear understanding of who you will serve and how you will be able to define and deliver what your clients want and need, will help you attract the right people at the right time.

Of course, you may work with whomever you choose; however, by narrowly defining your ideal client, you will be better able to find them, talk to them, and get hired. For example, if you are a Relationship coach who works with couples, it is easier to pursue couples who are empty nesters, or maybe those who have children at home, than attempt to target all couples. As another example, if you are a Business coach it's easier to search for dentists than it is to target all medical practitioners. By understanding your clients and their greatest struggles, you will start to communicate with them in ways that will attract them to your coaching services because they know you offer the help they need.

Your Ideal Client

Depending on the type of coaching and your area of focus, your ideal client could be an individual or a business. Each of these areas of focus "hears" differently. Understanding the details of their challenges and knowing what they are searching for can help you create the right programs, services and messaging to attract them.

By narrowly defining your clients, you will be successful in finding them. It may feel counterintuitive to limit, rather than to broaden your scope. However, the more specifically you can define your ideal client, the more business you will discover.

The following exercises provide the opportunity for you to work through individual and corporate perspectives. Choose the exercise(s) that are specific to your coaching practice. Spend some time with these exercises. Think about your ideal client and do the research to learn about them. Even if you plan to focus your efforts on organizations and teams, you need to identify the decision makers and their wants and needs.

Identify - Identify Your Ideal Client

Exercise - Identify Your Corporate Clients

Identify the industry and organizational information about your Ideal corporate clients. Include their challenges, wants and needs. Be as specific as possible.

Describe the industries you want to focus on.

Are they for profit and/or non-profit?

What are the biggest challenges affecting their employees or their team?

How does this affect their business growth or bottom line? Quantify, if possible.

Do they have a budget for coaching and/or training? If so, what would be the industry average?

Are you looking to facilitate team training or leadership coaching?

What training topics do they need that you can facilitate?

What value do you bring to the organization?

Name five organizations that represent your ideal client.

What is the title of the decision maker and their department, if known?

The Coach Business Guide

Exercise - Identify Your Individual Clients

Identify the challenges, wants and needs of those individuals you would like to coach. Be as specific as possible.

What are their demographics?
- Age
- Gender
- Marital Status
- Income Range
- Education
- Religious Affiliation
- Ethnicity
- Current Job Type (professional, blue collar, executive)
- Other

Where do they live, work and play?

What are the challenges that keep them up at night?

What is missing in their life or business?

What do they need? What are they looking for?

What might stop them from buying your services?

What will happen to them if they do not work with you?

Describe your ideal client. Be as specific as possible.

Write down five places where you might find your ideal client.

Identify - Identify Your Ideal Client

If you are able to finish the following sentence with absolute confidence, you are ready to move forward.

I am the perfect coach for _____ because I help them _____.

If you do not feel excited about working with your ideal client that you just described or you are still uncertain what they need and what you bring to the coaching relationship, spend additional time on these exercises. The more you know about your ideal client, the better. We will use this information as we develop your services and craft your messaging and work through your marketing plan later in the book.

Now that you have identified who you want to serve, it's time to determine how you will work with them.

6
Identify How You Will Work

There are so many ways to work with your ideal client! You will want to understand the different types of coaching and training experiences that can be created for your clients and where you see yourself being successful.

As you read these descriptions, identify which approaches will work best for you and the people you are helping. Spend time understanding the risks and benefits of each to make informed decisions about how you will work.

One-to-One

Most coaches include One-to-One coaching in their practice. For some, this may be the best way to get started. At a later time, you can expand into other approaches as you grow your coaching business.

The One-to-One coaching approach allows for intimacy, privacy, customization, flexibility, greater confidentiality, and a deeper long-term relationship. It can open up the door to other opportunities too, like team training. This type of coaching in the C-suite can be very lucrative.

Individual coaching can be done in most any setting -- in person, virtually, or even on the phone. There are text coaching platforms where you can easily communicate with your ideal client. You can set up automated reminders, pre-programmed messages, and track how your customers are progressing.

In the following table, you will see some risks and benefits of using One-to-One coaching as a business model. You may have other experiences that pertain specifically to you that should also be included.

Risks	Benefits
• Inability to keep your pipeline full • Limited revenue based on limited hours available • Higher price points may price you out of your market • Fewer prospects due to lack of corporate funding • Clients may be less committed • Lower retention rates • Cancellation can sabotage your income	• Build stronger relationships with your clients • Find open doors to more business • Flexibility in your schedule • Greater flexibility in your location with new technology options • Greater potential for referrals

One-to-Many

One-to-Many coaching provides an opportunity for you to engage with groups for a specific coaching or training topic. Examples of One-to-Many include workshops, team training, retreats or group coaching, all of which could be either in-per-

Identify - Identify How You Will Work

son, or online. You could also be working with smaller groups in multiple sessions with one of your coaching packages.

This approach provides flexibility in working and can open up the door for One-to-One coaching. It can provide opportunities for additional One-to-Many sessions as follow up and affords an organization the ability to work with you at a lower cost per person. Companies, schools and even churches will often budget for this type of group coaching and training.

By coaching this way, you can reach a larger audience of your ideal clients at a lower price point. This is especially beneficial with those unfamiliar or new to working with you. As with all coaching models, there are risks and benefits. We have defined some of them in the following table.

Risks	**Benefits**
<ul><li>Inability to manage the room</li><li>Technology challenges</li><li>Physical or virtual room constraints</li><li>Lack of privacy and intimacy</li><li>Inability to keep the group engaged over the length of the session</li><li>Upfront costs associated with the venue, if responsible</li><li>Ineffective marketing to fill the space</li><li>Less control of confidentiality</li></ul>	<ul><li>Broader reach with your brand</li><li>Ability to serve and help more people</li><li>Creates upsell potential for your services</li><li>Lucrative in the corporate arena</li></ul>

Online

Many coaches are making the transition to online coaching and training. Clients today are looking for flexibility, convenience and efficiency. Online coaching offers you the opportunity to coach and train anywhere, anytime, even from the beach! What really matters is how your clients want to engage with you. Here are some risks and benefits of coaching online.

Risks	Benefits
• Privacy concerns • Technology failures • Client technology discomfort • Client distractions • Added expense for technology	• Scheduling flexibility • Convenience • Eliminate travel time and expenses • Ability to coach anywhere, any time

Digital Training

Digital training is a great way for you to train once, record it, and package it for resale. This training is usually recorded and made available to your clients to use at their own pace. The idea is that you do the work once, then sell the replay. You can host this training on your website or on a Learning Management System (LMS) platform to give your client digital access.

In this type of training you will typically integrate presentation slides, worksheets, and exercises. Certain platforms provide clients access for questions and follow up. Be sure to know all the risks and benefits. We have listed some in the following table.

Identify - Identify How You Will Work

Risks	Benefits
• Unable to market to your target audience • High no show rate • Technology challenges • Low completion rate • Technology learning curve • High cost vs. low return • Limited follow up for relationship building	• Lower cost to consumer for increased sales • Greater market reach • Can be automated • Upsell additional training and coaching • Can be lucrative with the right product

Retreats

A retreat is a gathering of like-minded individuals coming together for a common learning or training experience. Usually, a retreat occurs over multiple days and is held on a weekend to accommodate a wider variety of clients' needs. Planning for a retreat takes a tremendous amount of upfront work to create the right environment, materials, accommodations, speakers, activities and exercises.

Attendees at a retreat are prime candidates for your coaching packages. While the retreat may not generate a profit, what you sell at the retreat can make it well worth the time and financial investment. Consider developing a retreat with other coaches or professionals who offer complimentary services or products. These joint ventures will allow you to share the work and the risk.

The Coach Business Guide

Hosting retreats comes with its own set of unique risks and rewards. We have highlighted some of them in the following table.

Risks	Benefits
• Higher upfront costs • Slow registration rates • Long preparation time • Cancellations • Low profit margins	• Opportunity to reach a larger audience • Upsell coaching packages and digital training • Networking • New strategic partnerships

Find the approach you are most comfortable with, either on-line or in-person. It sets the stage for you to focus on what you do best, coaching and training.

In the following exercise, you will be able to clearly understand how you see yourself working. You will also discover new ways to work with your clients for future expansion of your coaching practice.

Identify - Identify How You Will Work

Exercise - Identify How You Will Work

Answer the following to discover the different ways
in which you might serve your clients.

My ideal client is:

My coaching focus is:

Below, indicate which coaching approaches you will use and why. What percentage of your time will be spent operating in this approach?

One-to-One:

One-to-Many:

Online:

Digital Training:

Retreats:

What other possibilities did you discover to work with your ideal client?

Our goal for this section was for you to choose how you see yourself working with your ideal client. Did you discover the best way for you to work? Did you find new ways that you might work with them?

Examining the various ways that coaches often work, and understanding the risks and benefits involved, will help you make better decisions about your coaching practice. Repeat this exercise as needed for each area of focus.

Identify What is Important

This section, *Identify*, was designed to help you start to define your coaching practice. You were able to assess the skills and strengths you have that will make your business successful.

By documenting your calling, your vision and your beliefs, you should now be able to easily recognize what is important to you and why you want to have a coaching business. You also know who you want to serve and how you want to work with them. Narrowing down your focus and your ideal client will bring you additional business because of your clarity.

Let's start creating your processes and your packages!

Create

> *Create whatever causes a revolution in your heart.*
>
> - Elizabeth Gilbert

7
Your Coaching Process

The next step in establishing your business is to actually create what it looks like, what you are going to offer and how to get your first clients. Now that you have identified your ideal client, your focus and how you want to work, it is time to create your training, workshop or coaching packages.

In order to sell your services, you have to have something to sell. Understanding your processes will help you create your packages. The coaching packages, workshops and programs you create will represent you in the marketplace so you can attract new clients.

Process

Process refers to how you will coach, the materials you will use, and the flow you will follow as you guide your ideal client during their coaching journey. Coaching is not just a chit chat over coffee; it is having far deeper conversations that transform and effect change with your clients. These conversations do not just happen. You need to plan for them and create the materials you are going to use so that at the end of your time together, your client feels they have achieved their goals.

The Coach Business Guide

In this section, you will be looking at the processes you already have in place. You will also have the opportunity to use exercises that will lead you to creating your step-by-step plan that can be presented to a prospective client.

Ultimately, your process must be described to your prospective clients in a way that is clear and inviting, so they will want to work with you. Later, we will work on your messaging.

8
Before and After Transformation

Understanding your client's transformational journey is necessary to help them achieve success. Creating a "before" and "after" vision will help you develop your messaging and coaching materials. Your prospective client needs to see and feel where they are now, that you can relate to their challenges and understand what they are going through. Then, your client will begin to feel hope for what they could ultimately achieve. Finally, they need to get a glimpse of how you will get them there.

The Coach Business Guide

In the following exercises, you will identify the transformation that your ideal client will go through as they work with you.

Exercise - Client Transformation Journey

Describe where your ideal client is right now, and where you want them to be after working with you.

What are their challenges and struggles right now?

What beliefs do they have that are limiting their ability to move forward?

What are the impacts of their current frustrations on their life and/or business?

What will change for them as a result of working with you?

What will happen if they do not work with you?

Depending on your ideal client, complete the appropriate exercise. Remember, your corporate clients will be seeking a personal and business transformation.

Exercise - Personal Client Transformation

Describe the feelings that your client is having and how they will change after working with you.

How are they feeling right now emotionally?

How do they want to feel after coaching?

How will their lives and beliefs change?

Create - Before and After Transformation

> **Exercise - Corporate Client Transformation**
> Describe the feelings that your corporate client is having and how they will change after working with you.
>
> ---
>
> *What business objectives are they struggling to meet?*
>
> *What changes are they looking for in their team or staff?*
>
> *What organizational challenges need to be overcome?*
>
> *What negative emotions need to be considered?*
>
> *What positive organizational changes will occur from working with you?*

Were you able to get into the head of your ideal client? Do you understand the challenges that they face? Can you define the feelings they have associated with their struggles and challenges? Do you have a better sense of your part in their transformation journey? Whether it is an individual or a corporation, you must be able to describe what that transformation will be so you can speak in ways that will attract them to your services.

You absolutely must know what your ideal client is looking for on their journey, whether it is improving their team performance, finding a new job, or discovering a new purpose for their lives. People make decisions emotionally. In a person's decision-making process, they gather data and information, but it is emotion that makes them buy.

If you struggled with these exercises, work with your mentor or coach to help find the answers. Check our website at *www.CoachBusinessGuide.com* for more resources. You may need to do additional research, look at your competitors, or redefine your focus.

The Coach Business Guide

A clear understanding of the deep feelings that drive your ideal client's decision-making will help you gain business and get paid.

9
Define Your Materials

Perhaps you have been a coach for a while and already use certain exercises, worksheets and other intellectual property with your current clients. If so, leveraging these things could mean you are already halfway there!

Now's the time for you to review what you have and begin creating those materials you will need to help you in your coaching sessions and workshops. You may not have all the tools you need created yet, and that is okay! You may be surprised to discover how many free exercises and other resources that you can find online. There are also "white label" tools you can purchase for a nominal fee and add your company's branding or logo.

You may have completed certifications and training that allow you to duplicate their materials for use with your clientele. There may be some limitations or restrictions, so make sure you know what you can and cannot use or modify. You will also want to know if you can co-brand by putting your own logo on the material. Make sure you fully understand how the copyrighted material can be used. Seek the help of an attorney if needed.

> **Exercise - Define Your Materials**
>
> Make note of what you already have available
> and have the legal right to use.
>
> ---
>
> Create a list of any worksheets or content that you have created on your own.
>
> Create a list of exercises that you want to use with your clients.
>
> What assessment tools are you trained in and have access to?
>
> What materials from your certification programs are you able to use?
>
> What video or audio programs do you have to work with?
>
> What workshop materials have you developed or have access to?
>
> What slide decks and presentation material do you have access to?
>
> What content do you have from any other source that you can use?

Are you finding that you have gaps in the materials needed to properly work with your clients? Have you discovered that you have more than you even knew? Do you see patterns or similarities emerging with the items you already have available to use in your coaching practice? Do the materials align with the focus of your business?

If you struggled in this area, do not despair! You will be able to use the exercises later in this section to help you define and create what you need. Be sure to check out our website at *www.CoachBusinessGuide.com* for additional resources.

10
Creating a Basic Workshop

You may decide to pursue workshops or training sessions and target corporations, non-profits organizations, or groups of individuals. Examples include online group training, retreats, Mastermind sessions or Lunch 'n Learn events. For the sake of simplicity, we will call any group session a "workshop."

Throughout the next exercises, you will create a basic workshop that will be the foundation of your offerings. You will be able to customize it later with each client.

Workshop Basic Information

If you have never created a workshop before, you will need to imagine your audience so that you can start to define the expectations of their experience. Refer back to the Exercises - Defining Your Focus, Identify Your Corporate Clients and Identify Your Individual Clients to answer these questions.

> ## Exercise - Workshop Basic Information
> Gather some basic information by answering the following questions.
>
> What is the topic of your training?
>
> Write a short description about your audience.
>
> How many attendees will you typically have?
>
> What specific challenges are you addressing?
>
> How much time will you need to present your material?
>
> How many breakout sessions will you have?
>
> What breaks or meals do you need to include?

Workshop Objectives and Outcomes

In order to create a workshop, it is essential that you know the objectives and the outcome your attendees are expecting. Focus on what your ideal client's most pressing challenges are and you will be able to create a foundational offering that can be changed based on each individual client's needs.

Create - Creating a Basic Workshop

> ### Exercise - Workshop Objectives and Outcomes
>
> List the objectives and outcomes your ideal client could expect.
>
> ---
>
> *What specific objectives do you expect to accomplish through this workshop?*
>
> *What outcomes will your ideal client experience through participating?*
>
> *At the end of the workshop, what changes can your client anticipate?*
>
> *How will they measure and evaluate the success of your workshop?*
>
> *What support within the organization is needed to reinforce your training?*
>
> *How will you know you have met their objectives?*

Workshop Materials and Exercises

In any workshop, you will likely incorporate pre-work materials and exercises. These may be worksheets, assessments or other handouts that enhance the experience and deepen the learning. You can use this information in your materials to create engaging slides for your presentation. It will take time to develop materials that will guide your training sessions toward the outcomes you are promising, so be patient.

The following exercise will help you identify materials you have, as well as the things you need to gather or create.

Exercise - Workshop Materials and Exercises

Identify the materials you will need to deliver the workshop or training.

What core materials will you use?

What pre-work will you require?

Do you need to create a slide deck?

Have you got a script or outline?

What audio or visuals will you be using?

What materials do you need to create or obtain?

Workshop Follow Up Planning

Determine how you will follow up at the end of your workshop. A few examples of how to close your presentation include providing a survey, asking your clients to write a testimonial about your services, or inviting them to check out other services you offer.

Create - Creating a Basic Workshop

Use the following exercise to identify what follow up activities you will use to continue to engage and develop long-term relationships with attendees.

Exercise - Workshop Follow Up Planning

Complete the following to know what you need to do after the workshop is completed.

What are the next steps for attendees? What are they committing to?

Do you have a feedback form or survey created?

Do you have post-training work planned?

What additional business do you want from your client?

Are you scheduling complementary one-to-one conversations with participants?

What is the next step for you to follow up with the decision maker?

Workshop Name

What's in a name? Most workshops or trainings have a name, and you have choices on how much information to provide. The name should be descriptive enough that the prospective client gets a hint at what you are offering. Here are some sample workshop names:

> *Communication for Engineers*

> *Diversity Training for Teams*

> *Driving Future Growth through Your Executive Team*

> *Developing Optimum Team Strategies Workshop*

> *Building Engagement for Teams*

> *Strengths Based Parenting to Build Your Family*

> *Branding for Beginners*

> *Path to a Healthful Life*

As you can see, you have a lot of flexibility in naming your workshop. Once you have a list of ideas, share with friends, family and other coaches to get feedback.

Exercise - Workshop Name
Brainstorm some names for your workshop and write them down.

Create - Creating a Basic Workshop

Workshop Description

Once you have a name that attracts your ideal client, your description will then provide information about the workshop and the outcomes you expect to provide. This draws them in to learn more about your services. Your description must touch their pain points and convey the promise of a solution. They need to feel that they can move forward in their journey by working with you.

Your brief description needs to be short, clear and concise. It should include what will happen, what your ideal client will achieve and over what length of time. Here are a few examples of what other coaches have used:

"Diversity Training for Teams is designed to bring greater understanding and awareness to the complex issues of our day. This two-session training will improve communication and collaboration and give a clear process for handling challenging conversations."

"Strengths Based Parenting to Build Your Family will help you fall in love with your kids again! Join us for this three-week series and learn how to focus on your child's God-given strengths to motivate and inspire them to be their best."

Later, we will spend some time developing your messaging to promote your business and your offerings. Right now, we are focusing on nailing down the basic elements of what you offer.

> ### Exercise - Workshop Description
> Answer the following to write a description about your workshop or training program.
>
> ---
>
> *What is the name of your workshop?*
>
> *How long is your workshop?*
>
> *Who are you serving?*
>
> *What are the objectives and outcomes they will achieve?*
>
> *Write a basic description of your workshop in a few sentences using your responses from the previous exercises and those you just answered above.*

There are a lot of exercises in this chapter and you were pushed into creating a foundation for your basic workshop! Recognize that each specific client will have unique needs that will require you to customize your offerings to meet their goals and objectives. Do you see now that you have enough information to craft a basic workshop? Were you able to determine what materials you have available that can be used or adapted for a variety of workshops and trainings?

Often, we skimp on thinking about the follow up until after a workshop is over. Taking time now to develop, describe and create the necessary materials and follow up to engage your clients will help ensure future business. Be sure to share your work with your peer coaches, mentors or other support people to capture feedback, suggestions and ideas.

Now that you have gathered the essentials to planning your own workshop, you will need to map out the session flow and how much time you will spend on each component. We will guide you through this in the next chapter.

11
Mapping Out Your Workshop

Mapping out the time allotted for you to deliver the content and exercises in your workshop will allow you to meet the objectives. You need to ensure that you know what will happen from the moment you walk in the door until the very end of your training.

We have identified four basic components that are generally included in every workshop. We will cover each and offer an example. In the exercise following this section, you will map out your own workshop.

Workshop Session Introductions and Objectives

You will begin every workshop by introducing yourself, letting your attendees know the objectives and general flow of the day. Here is where you will add an icebreaker, or other exercises to kick off your time together.

Core Materials, Exercises and Discussion

Plan the segments for your presentation and determine what core material you will cover. You will need to develop an outline, a script and any slides or handouts that you will use to reinforce your material. Lay out any discussion topics, exercises, pre-work/assessments, breakout sessions or other planned activities to be integrated with your material. Include group conversations to enable your participants to ask questions and engage with the material and with one another.

Action Plan

At the end of each workshop, asking your clients to create a personalized action plan will allow them to engage with the workshop concepts after you are gone. It enables them to make a commitment to move forward and deepen their understanding and make changes to help them meet their objectives. Including a specific timeframe for each action step will help the participants successfully incorporate the new training into their organization.

Summary Conversation

At the end of most workshops, there should be a conversation summarizing the day, what was learned, and key takeaways. Begin with some examples or invite your audience to provide input. Include a survey, asking your participants to provide feedback, suggestions and ideas regarding the workshop. If appropriate, share information about your other services and invite participants to move into another program or training that you offer.

Finally, at the end of each workshop, be sure to schedule a follow up session with your client to share the survey feedback, and other suggestions and ideas you have as a result of the training.

Create - Mapping Out Your Workshop

Workshop Timeline Flow

Each of these basic components need to be mapped out for your workshop to fit within the time allotted. Here's an example of how we have mapped out a half-day workshop.

Workshop Timeline Flow

Time Allotment	Basic Component	Description	Materials Needed
20 Min	Introduction, Overview and Objectives	Review agenda and objectives. Icebreaker exercise to create community and authenticity.	Slides and presentation script. Ice Breaker exercise: Words Matter
30 Min	Core Materials, Exercises and Discussion	Introduction to the 4 communication styles.	Slides and presentation script. Handout: Understanding the 4 Communication Styles
60 Min	Core Materials, Exercises and Discussion	Assessment review and how to use your communication style in day to day interactions	Slides & presentation script. Handout: Communication Style Assessment Results for each participant
10 Min	BREAK		

Workshop Timeline Flow Continued

Time Allotment	Basic Component	Description	Materials Needed
60 Min	Core Materials, Exercises and Discussion	Breakout session: Complimentary Communication Styles and how to interact	Breakout materials, slides, flip charts and pens Handout: Complimentary Communication Styles exercise
10 Min	BREAK		
30 Min	Core Materials, Exercises and Discussion	Communication Conflict	Slides and presentation script Handout: Handling Communication Conflict
15 Min	Action Plan	Participants will create their own individualized action plan to drive commitment for application of core concepts.	Slides and presentation script Handout: Action Plan Template
15 Min	Summary Conversation	Participants share personal takeaways and "aha moments". Distribute participant survey. Schedule follow up with the team leader.	Flip Chart and Pen Handout: Workshop Survey Form

Create - Mapping Out Your Workshop

Now, it is your turn to map out your basic workshop session based on your ideal timing (4-hours, full day or multi-day training) to make sure you meet your ideal client's objectives. Using the following exercise, fill in the information to determine how you will spend the time allotted for your basic workshop.

Exercise - Mapping Out Your Workshop

Using the information gathered from the previous chapter, use your journal to plan your training or workshop.

Make sure each of the components are included, if appropriate. The components to choose from are: **Introduction, Overview and Objectives, Core Material, Discussion and Exercises, Action Plan, and Summary Conversation.**

Time Allotment	Basic Component	Description	Materials Needed

Where did you struggle as you worked through these exercises? Do you see gaps you need to fill? Will your materials and session flow meet the objectives of your ideal client? What materials do you need to develop?

As you now know, there is more to creating a workshop than meets the eye. It is necessary preparation to ensure that you meet your ideal client's needs and provide an effective presentation. Gathering information, developing materials and creating your workshop session flow in advance will ensure success.

Following your session flow, you can develop your script or outline that you can use during your training. You can also use it to create your slide deck and any handouts you will use. Be sure to also design your end-of-workshop survey to invite participants to provide feedback, suggestions and ideas.

Throughout the rest of the book, you will use this information to build your messaging and reach new clients.

12

Creating a One-to-One Coaching Package

Now that you have a deeper understanding of your ideal client's journey, it is time to put that into a coaching package. No coach wants to do a single coaching session with a client. Your goal should be to create a long term commitment through your One-to-One coaching packages. With a multi-session approach, you will be able to help your clients transform and reach their goals and provide a stable income for your business.

There are advantages to packaging your services. A package sets an expectation on how long you and your client will work together, enables you to create topic-specific sessions, and helps you determine what materials to use.

You need to plan your coaching package so that you take your client through a step-by-step process to help them achieve their goals. You want to deepen your ideal client's relationship and engagement with you. Your prospects will want to know that there is a beginning and end that will get them the results they want.

The Coach Business Guide

The following information and exercises will help you create a basic coaching package that you can adapt and change as needed. Having your basic package developed will give you material you can use to communicate what you offer to your ideal client.

Package Basic Information

If you have never created a coaching package, you will need to imagine working with your ideal client to define the expectations of their experience. In the next exercise, you will capture basic information to guide you.

Exercise - Package Basic Information
Answer the following to identify the basic components your package will provide.

What is your area of focus for the package?

Who is your ideal client?

What are their greatest challenges?

How long will each session last?

How many coaching sessions will you need to provide the client's desired outcomes?

How will you communicate with your client throughout the length of the coaching sessions?

What access will your client have to you between sessions?

Package Objectives and Outcomes

Before you can create a package, you need to understand your ideal client's objectives for hiring a coach. With this knowl-

Create - Creating a One-to-One Coaching Package

edge, you will be able to provide and achieve the outcomes they seek with your coaching package. By focusing on their most pressing challenges, you will be able to create a foundational coaching package that can be changed based on each individual client's needs. Completing the next exercise will help you gain clarity about what outcomes your ideal client expects.

Exercise - Package Objectives and Outcomes

Answer the following to identify your ideal client's objectives and expectations.

What specific objectives do you expect to accomplish through your coaching package?

What outcomes will your ideal client experience?

At the end of your package sessions, what changes can your client anticipate?

How will your client measure and value the success of your coaching?

How will you know you have met your client's objectives?

Package Materials Needed

Perhaps you have been a coach for a while, and already use certain exercises, worksheets and other intellectual property with your current clients. If so, leveraging these things could mean you are already halfway there! If you have not, you will need to refer back to the Exercise - Define Your Materials. You may also decide that you need to create new materials.

The next exercise will allow you to think through the materials you will be using in your sessions. If you find yourself lacking in materials, exercises or worksheets, check our website at *www.CoachBusinessGuide.com* for ideas and information.

Exercise - Package Materials Needed
From your core list of materials, determine what you will need for your coaching package.

Is there any pre-work material to be completed by the client prior to the first session?

List materials or handouts you will use.

What materials do you need to develop?

List exercises you will utilize.

Will you incorporate video or audio programs?

Will there be homework or action steps to be taken between sessions?

Package Follow Up Planning

The final session of any coaching package needs to include a way for you to continue the relationship with your ideal client. This is the perfect opportunity to explore another coaching package or service that you offer.

You might provide a survey or some type of measurement for your client to evaluate and confirm that the objectives were achieved. You may ask for testimonials and provide a way for them to share their experience. This would also be the time to ask for referrals. The next exercise will help you plan your final session and keep your business moving forward.

Create - Creating a One-to-One Coaching Package

> ### Exercise - Package Follow Up Planning
> Answer the following to help identify what you will include in the final session of your coaching package.
>
> *How will you survey your clients for feedback?*
>
> *How will you collect testimonials?*
>
> *What will you use to collect referrals?*
>
> *What coaching package or services can you offer next?*
>
> *How will you communicate with the client after the coaching package ends?*

Package Individual Session Focus

Earlier in the book, you identified the transformational journey you wanted for your ideal client. In a coaching package, that journey will be divided into individual sessions. Looking back at your objectives, determine how many sessions you will need in order to meet your client's expectations. For some coaches, this will be three or four sessions. For others, it could be monthly sessions for a full year.

In the following example, we show what an individual coaching session could look like.

Package Individual Session Focus Example

Session Focus	Introduction and getting started.
Objective	Discover where the client is, roadblocks to success, and exploration of the best career path. Establish expectations for subsequent sessions.
Desired Outcome	Client has a clear understanding of program and expectations. Seeking new job in automobile sector.
Homework	Take CSF and VIA assessments. Sign up for Indeed.
Materials Needed	Client intake form; probing questions
Exercises	9-minute Clarity Exercise for Big Why
Plan Next Steps	Schedule midweek text check-in to verify action to scan job boards. Book all subsequent appointments.

By mapping out what you plan to do in each session, you will be able to ensure that your clients reach their goals. Remember, you will adapt your basic coaching package based on each of your client's individual needs.

Create - Creating a One-to-One Coaching Package

In the next exercise, create the focus of each individual session in your package. In the last session, remember to incorporate a way to capture feedback, testimonials and offer the next coaching package.

Exercise: Package Individual Session Focus

Map out each of the sessions in your package. Use the material from the earlier exercises to identify the session focus, objective, outcome, materials, exercises and next steps.

Note that your final session should include opportunities for referrals, testimonials and new business. Duplicate for each session in your package.

Session Focus	
Objective	
Desired Outcome	
Homework	
Materials Needed	
Exercises	
Plan Next Steps	
Final Session Opportunities for Feedback	
Testimonials and Upsell	

The Coach Business Guide

Package Name

Most coaching packages have a name that will attract your ideal client. The name will capture their attention and draw them in. It should be just descriptive enough that your prospective client gets a hint at what you are offering. You want your potential and existing clients to see that you are offering solutions to meet their needs.

Here are some examples of names for different kinds of coaching packages. Notice that the name implies the problem and the solution.

> *Bust Your Stress and Gain Your Sanity Back! program*

> *Upgrade Your Career package*

> *Restore Your Health and Life Balance package*

> *Launch Your Business in Six Weeks program*

> *Managing Family, Life and Career Coaching package*

> *Transform Your Marriage to Last a Lifetime program*

As you can see, there can be quite a bit of diversity in naming your coaching package. Once you have a list of ideas, share with potential clients, friends, family and other coaches to get feedback.

Now it is time to create your own. Complete the following exercise in your journal.

Exercise - Package Name
Brainstorm some names for your coaching package and write them down.

Create - Creating a One-to-One Coaching Package

Package Description

Describing your coaching package in terms that can convey what it is and how it works will attract prospective clients. They will see the name of your package, and then seek more information. Your description must touch their pain points and convey the promise of a solution. They need to feel that they can move forward in their journey by working with you.

Your brief description needs to be short, clear and concise. It should include what will happen, what your ideal client will achieve and over what length of time. Here are a few examples of what other coaches have used:

> *"In the 6-week Uplevel Your Career package, you will discover your strengths and skills, explore new possibilities and determine obstacles that are getting in your way of advancement. Create your own career plan and level up!"*

> *"With the Launch Your Business in 6-Weeks program, you will finally reach your dream of starting your own company! Our process will break through the stumbling blocks and help identify your interest, determine your goals, and focus your energy on those critical steps to make that dream come true."*

The next exercise will help you nail down the basic elements of what you offer in two or three sentences. Later, we will spend some time developing your messaging to promote your business and your offerings.

The Coach Business Guide

> ## Exercise - Package Description
> Answer the following to write a description about your coaching package.
>
> ---
>
> What is the name of your package?
>
> How many sessions are in your package and over what timeframe?
>
> What are the basic objectives and outcomes your client can anticipate?
>
> Write a basic description of your package in a few sentences using your responses from the previous exercises and those you answered above.

Package Examples

Here is an example of a six session career coaching package to help clients in their job search. Notice that we have mapped out each session and what we plan to accomplish with our imaginary client.

> *Ideal Client:* A woman in the automobile industry looking for upper level management advancement.
>
> *Objectives and Outcomes:* For this six session package, we will focus on identifying the client's new career objectives and getting a new job.
>
> *Package Name:* Uplevel Your Career!
>
> *Package Description:* In the 6-week Uplevel Your Career package, you will discover your strengths and skills, explore new possibilities and determine obstacles that are getting in your way of advancement. Create your own career plan and level up!

Create - Creating a One-to-One Coaching Package

Session Focus and Materials Needed: *6 weekly sessions of 60 minutes.*

1. **Career Fact Finding Session** - *Discover where the client is, roadblocks to success, and exploration of the best career path. Establish expectations for the five subsequent sessions.*

2. **Career Strengths and Skill Inventory** - *Identify past experience, skill set and strengths that will be used to identify opportunities. Use Inventory exercise and add skills assessments.*

3. **Career Exploration** - *Discover blocks that are preventing progress and causing client to be stuck. Client to identify what they want in their career, what creates satisfaction and where they see themselves working and serving.*

4. **Career Advancement Possibilities** - *Explore different paths and new ideas, helping client think outside the box for new possibilities.*

5. **Career Prioritizing** - *Talk through options, narrow focus and make a choice. Help client ensure this focus is in alignment with goals and objectives. Determine the best career target goal, create research plan and identify potential obstacles.*

6. **Career Action Plan** - *Create an action plan with next steps to get their ideal job.*

Next Steps: *Mid-week check-in via text during 6 weeks. Sell additional Job Search Coaching Package for resume development and interview skills.*

It is now time to map out your coaching package. Use the example as a model and refer back to prior exercises for the information you need.

Exercise: Mapping Your One-to-One Package

Use the following as a template to organize the content of your coaching package. Complete for as many sessions as needed.

Ideal Client:

Objectives and Outcomes:

Package Name:

Package Description:

Session Focus and Materials Needed:

Session Descriptions:

Session 1

Session 2

Session 3

Next Steps:

Where did you struggle as you worked through the exercise? Do you see gaps you need to fill? Will your materials and session focus meet the objectives of your ideal client? Check in with another coach or your mentor for suggestions and ideas if needed.

Create - Creating a One-to-One Coaching Package

Spend time planning and developing your content, materials and the focus of your sessions in order to create a transformational experience for your ideal client. It is always good to be prepared and let your passion flow through your session. Planning brings confidence.

13

Some Assembly Required

Now that we have walked through the basics of what you will be offering your clients, you will find that there is still some work to be done. You may have worksheets to create or exercises to modify.

You also need to prepare before each session or training so you are ready to give your clients your complete attention. Here are a few additional things you might need to think about before each session starts.

Tools and Resources

With each session or training, you will want to have worksheets or other tools you need on hand and ready to use.

You may be intuitive and less formal in your approach and be able to identify what tools you need in the moment. Having an easily accessible resource sheet listing your exercises and tools will allow you to avoid searching for materials during the session.

Every time you deliver your courses or have a coaching session with a client, there may be additional costs, such as assessment tools, worksheets or third-party materials. Printing could be an added expense as well. Identifying all of these items up front will help you be more profitable.

Probing Questions

Similar to having worksheets and work prepared for the client prior to your session, preparing questions for exploration during the session is helpful. These could be conversation starters, or things you want to ask from previous sessions to check for new challenges or new opportunities. Having a few questions jotted down before your client arrives will give you confidence and a possible direction for your conversations.

Flexibility

One thing you will want to be prepared for is getting completely derailed from your planned session by your client! Coaches are always at the service of their clients' needs. Often the best laid plans run amok because of a change in their client's life. Just remember to stay fluid and flexible so that you can adapt to changing circumstances.

Competition

Knowing what your competition is offering and the fees they are charging can give you insight into what the market expects. Coaching organizations can be a wealth of information on how to price your services and packages.

Do an online search to see what other coaches or training companies in your area are charging for similar services. Some things to look for: who is offering similar services, how do they describe their packages and what are they charging? You can also talk to other coaches, to uncover what is being offered in your area. Compare package and workshop descriptions to see what market advantage they are focusing on. Understand

Create - Some Assembly Required

their value proposition and determine what you offer that is different, better or gives you an edge.

Use this information to help you identify untapped opportunities that align with what you offer and develop the appropriate pricing for your coaching packages and workshops.

Time Commitment

Whatever your program, workshop or package includes, be sure to calculate the total time commitment you will need to invest in order to make it successful. Remember to include any pre- and post-work to better understand how much time will be needed.

Follow Up

Following up with your clients after your training or coaching package is complete will allow you to continue building your relationship. There are other opportunities you may not yet be aware of to work with them further. Long term follow up methods will create "touch points" and prompts to bring you back to mind. By offering resources and information of interest, you will maintain these connections and be the first person they think of and call when they need help.

14

Pricing

"How much do I charge?" is a common question coaches ask. Pricing is one of the most challenging decisions you will make for your coaching business. Often, coaches undervalue themselves and tend to price their work and what they do at a much lower rate than what is possible.

Many coaches "spiritualize" money because they feel "called" to coach in order to help people, not to get rich. Then, they find themselves feeling guilty when charging. Conversations about payment for your services may be difficult and awkward.

Packaging your coaching services will help, because you are no longer just charging an hourly rate. Instead, you are showing your clients how you can help them and what they will achieve. People pay for outcomes.

There is a client for every price point. Charging too little is not a competitive advantage; in fact, underpricing can be perceived as less valuable. The truth is this: you will only charge for your services what you believe in your mind you are worth. By working with a coach on your limiting beliefs about money, you will likely make better decisions about pricing your programs.

Be bold and confident and charge fair market value right from the beginning. Raising your fees at a later date can be difficult for current clients. Price right the first time!

In the next exercise, you will begin gathering information to help you determine your pricing.

Create - Pricing

Exercise - Pricing Your Coaching Package or Workshop

Use the following as a guide to determine the pricing for your package or workshop.

Package/Workshop Name:

Number of Participants:

Number of Sessions:

Time length of each Session:

Competitor Pricing:

Total Time Commitment:
Development (materials, script, slide deck, etc.)
Session Prep (transportation, material adjustments)
Session (total time for workshop or sessions)
Post-work (follow up communication)

Facility/Technology Costs:

Materials Costs:

Promotion Costs:

Support/Staff Costs:

What is the price you want to charge for the value you offer?

Less your total costs/expenses?

Net income for workshop or coaching package:

Did these exercises help you to clearly determine what costs and time commitments need to be included in your pricing? Were you able to determine the actual net income for each workshop or coaching package you offer? Are you comfortable with the price you have established?

Remember, you will only charge as much as your mind will allow you to charge. Do you feel confident in the amount you will be asking for your workshops or coaching packages? Can you pass on business that brings in a lesser rate?

Creating Confidence

Creating your basic offering will give you confidence. With the material you have developed in this section, you will be able to customize your workshops and coaching packages to meet your ideal client's unique goals. Return again and again as your coaching practice grows and develop new ways to help your clients solve their challenges.

If at any time you are uncomfortable with what you have developed, reach out to your support team for feedback. Taking the time now to create this material will help you become successful.

Plan

> *Good fortune is what happens when opportunity meets with planning.*
>
> - Thomas Edison

15

Planning for Your Financial Success

Now that you have created your basic coaching package or workshop, it is time to incorporate the financial aspects into your overall business objectives. Establishing a financial plan is going to help you create a thriving coaching practice. It will help you understand exactly what you need to do to be financially successful.

You may be tempted to skip this section. Please don't. As mentioned earlier, many coaches "spiritualize" money and avoid planning for their financial success. As a result, they never develop a thriving coaching practice. Thinking through the money aspects of your business may be the most difficult task in your path to success. You need money to grow and develop and you won't have enough unless you plan for it. There can be financial benefits to starting your own business and this is where a financial or tax advisor can provide guidance and help.

The Coach Business Guide

To understand your financial goals, you need to evaluate several variables. These include the hours you have available, the income you want to earn, and the basic expenses you are already paying. As you go through this process, you may find times when you just do not have the answers. This is when you can turn to your legal and financial resources, as well as your support team for help.

Throughout this section, you will find exercises to help you fully recognize your business objectives by understanding expenses, investment and your time commitment.

16

Work Week

Let's start by mapping out what your work week will look like. As you consider how much time you can commit to your practice, recognize that there are operational tasks you will need to cover to ensure you achieve a successful business. Session preparation, research, workshop/product creation, networking, marketing, and lead generation will likely take 50% of your available work hours. Schedule follow up, marketing and administrative tasks during non-coaching hours.

You might have to incorporate travel time to actually coach your clients or facilitate a workshop. Working across time zones will also impact your time commitments. It is really easy to overlook the amount of time that these tasks will take to establish and run your coaching practice.

Be honest and real about how many hours you can invest in your business. You already have commitments to family, friends, volunteer activities, and so forth. The next exercise will help you capture what obligations you have to get clear on your time available to coach and train.

Exercise - Time Available

Document where your time is already allocated.

What kind of family obligations do you need to schedule each week?

How many hours a week can you dedicate to the administration of your business?

How many hours a week are you available to coach?

If money were not an issue, what tasks would you outsource now?

Blocking your calendar with family obligations and administration time will help you see the remaining time you have available to actually coach. Were you surprised by the limited amount of time you have available to coach?

Whether you plan to coach part time or full time, taking control of your calendar is an important step to staying on track.

17

Investment and Income Needs

If you are running a coaching business, you need to be realistic about the money you want to earn. You may have a job you are trying to replace, or you may be looking for supplemental income. Maybe you are looking for a career change or even thinking about coaching as part of your retirement plan. Establishing your financial goals upfront will set the stage for you to plan what activities you need to do to achieve your objectives.

There is a wide range of start-up costs. Some things are "must haves" and others are not essential for launching your business. Many business advisors suggest a minimum of $5000 will be spent in the first year. In reality, though, you can be up and running on a shoestring and spread some of those expenses out over time.

Some examples of start-up costs that you may incur include state filing fees, opening a business bank account, creating business cards and other marketing collateral. At some point, you may choose to hire an attorney or accountant. You may also need a video platform for virtual coaching.

Complete the following exercise to get a better understanding of your investment and income needs.

> ## Exercise - Investment and Income Needs
> Identify your investment funds and income needed.
>
> *How much money do you have to invest for monthly recurring business expenses?*
>
> *How much money do you have right now to invest for any start-up costs?*
>
> *How much gross income do you want or need to earn each month?*
>
> *Do you have other income to help supplement your living expenses while you build your business? If so, how much?*

Current Expenses

There are a few basic expenses that begin right from the start. Some of these you may already be paying for out of your personal budget. Your phone, a computer and the Internet are really all you need to get started. Documenting these expenses will allow you to establish a baseline, even if you are allocating funds from your personal account.

In the following exercise, you will be able to see these costs on paper, which will give you a greater view into what monetary commitments you already have and what you will need monthly to support yourself financially.

Plan - Investment and Income Needs

Exercise - Current Expenses

Document the services you already pay for that can be used in your business. Write the amount you are currently paying.

Phone:

Internet:

Video Platform:

Other Services or Platforms:

Determining Your Income

You priced your coaching package or workshop earlier in the book. You will use that information to calculate your estimated annual income.

There are a variety of ways that you can earn revenue. As you think about your coaching practice, you can have a mix of services that you offer that will meet your income goals. Your coaching practice can include retreats, one-to-one coaching, group training, or other programs you develop.

In the example, we chose $50,000 as an annual revenue goal. We used sample pricing for workshops and coaching sessions based on what other coaches have told us they charge. We also calculated what our estimated annual expenses might be to help determine how the revenue goal could be achieved. By altering these numbers based on your own goals and coaching fees, you can create different pathways to reach your financial objectives.

The Coach Business Guide

Example for Determining Your Annual Income

Desired Annual Revenue	$50,000
Workshop Revenue	
# of workshops	6
$ per workshop	$4,000
Total Workshop Revenue	$24,000
Coaching Package Revenue	
# of packages	19 six-session packages (114)
$ per package	$899
Total Package Revenue	$17,081
1-to-1 Sessions	
# of sessions	82
$ per session	$150
Total Session Revenue	$12,240
Total Coaching Revenue	$53,321
Less Estimated Expenses	-$3,240
Estimated Total Annual Revenue	$50,081

Notes and Observations

Coaching fees vary widely. You may charge a higher or lower rate. Selling more coaching packages can provide a greater confidence in your revenue stream.

Plan - Investment and Income Needs

In the example, we have shown that there are numerous methods to generate revenue. There can be a lot of flexibility in the ways you earn your money. If your time is limited and you are able to gain additional workshop revenue, you can lower the number of One-to-One coaching sessions. If you prefer individual coaching, you will need to increase your number of coaching packages and one-to-one coaching.

Now it is your turn to get your numbers down on paper! Use the information from previous exercises regarding your time and package or workshop pricing to calculate how you will reach your annual revenue goals. Play with the calculations to determine what is realistic and feasible given the amount of time you have and the amount of money you are going to charge for your services.

Exercise - Determining Your Income

Refer to the *Exercises - Time Available and Pricing Your Coaching Package or Workshop* to determine the path to your desired annual revenue.

Desired Annual Revenue	$
Workshop Revenue	
# of workshops	
$ per workshop	$
Total Workshop Revenue	$
Coaching Package Revenue	
# of packages	
$ per package	$
Total Package Revenue	$
1-to-1 Sessions	
# of sessions	
$ per session	$
Total Session Revenue	$
Total Coaching Revenue	$
Less Estimated Expenses	-
Estimated Total Annual Revenue	$

Plan - Investment and Income Needs

Did you find any surprises as you worked through these exercises? Look at the numbers that you calculated. Are they realistic given the time you have available for coaching practice as well as your marketing and follow up efforts?

The intention of these exercises is to help you get an overview of your income needs and your current expenses. It is also to give you a dose of reality. You may have a goal that cannot be achieved yet because of a misalignment between your time available, your pricing and the amount of prospects you currently have. Many coaches are trying to replace an income. Just recognize that it will take time to build your practice and market your services to reach your desired financial goals.

Later, we will help you determine what other services you may need to create an accurate budget.

Plan Now to Reap the Rewards

There is a wealth of information in this section that will help ensure the success of your coaching practice. By doing your homework now and taking the time to identify your costs and revenue opportunities, you will be able to focus on profitable business prospects. If you struggle, we strongly recommend and encourage you to work with a mentor or business associate who can help you with the numbers.

You will be tempted to lower your prices or accept business proposals that do not fit your financial strategy. There are times where it may be advantageous to do so, but pay attention to your calculations before accepting a "better than nothing" deal.

Return often to this section as you develop new workshops and packages. As your coaching business grows, you will be making new investments that will impact your bottom line. Review this information several times a year and make adjustments as appropriate.

Launch

> *There's always time to launch your dreams.*
>
> - Maat Morrison

18
Getting Ready to Launch

It is almost time to launch your practice. You just have a few more things to do and you will be ready to hang your shingle!

You have done so much work developing and acknowledging yourself and your unique skill set, as well as building up a greater understanding of your ideal client. You know who they are and how you want to serve them. Your coaching package or workshop is ready to go to help your client with their transformational journey. You have also worked hard to establish a firm understanding your finances and have priced your packages and workshops to help you achieve profitability and your income goals.

In this section, we will focus on your messaging so that you attract your ideal client and help them learn about your services. They need to see how you can help them in their transformational journey.

We will also cover some of the legalities in officially launching your coaching business. There will be additional research and steps to take and you may need professional help.

Finally, we will guide you in getting your first clients. This will include tools that will help you, such as scheduling, virtual coaching, building your basic online presence and developing other messaging needs.

19

Package and Workshop Messaging

Messaging is about how to get people to buy your services. How you describe what you are offering will determine how you will reach and attract your best clients. In the next several exercises, we are going to break down the language that you will be able to use as a script when you are actually writing to or speaking with your prospective clients. This will give you confidence when discussing how you help people, what processes you use, the results they can expect and what it is like to work with you.

This messaging should paint word pictures for the people you talk to about your packages, your training and your coaching practice. It is not about one sentence or one paragraph. You will want to create multiple examples that you will use, depending on where you are and to whom you are speaking.

Keywords

As we start work on your messaging, the first step is to identify the best words to use to communicate with your clients. The words you use matter. They will either attract or repel potential clients. Identifying the words that are familiar to your clientele will allow them to hear you.

Find a quiet space and re-read what you wrote about your ideal client and their transformational journey, your focus area, your expertise, and your basic workshop or coaching package. You want to begin broadly, then narrow as you go.

Through the next exercises, you will drill down into those words your ideal client needs to hear. Look at your competitors, interview people, search online, talk to business professionals in the industry you have chosen to build your messaging vocabulary.

Exercise - Keyword Brainstorm
Brainstorm different words and phrases that will resonate with your ideal client.

Words or phrases that:

Describe your ideal client's challenges and pain points:

Describe the solutions you offer:

Create emotional connection:

Provide inspiration:

Motivate:

Refer to their industry:

Refer to your focus area:

Your client is using to search the internet for help:

Launch - Package and Workshop Messaging

> **Exercise - Keyword Selections**
>
> Narrow your word selection and create phrases using the words from Exercise - Keyword Brainstorm.
>
> *1. Circle those words that really jump off the page and resonate with you and write them below.*
>
> *2. Begin creating phrases with the words you have circled that will resonate with your ideal client and their challenges.*
>
> *3. Test out this new vocabulary and these new phrases with friends and family. Do they fit your practice well when describing the solutions you offer?*

Did you struggle to find the right words that your ideal client is wanting to hear? If so, you may need to do additional research or get clarity about their challenges and needs. Is the list of words and phrases you have discovered in alignment with you and how you want to serve?

You will be using these words and phrases as we work through your key messaging, package descriptions and marketing materials later.

20

Creating Your Key Messaging

We have broken down your key messaging into six short segments. These will enable you to better see and understand what your ideal client needs to hear so that they are motivated to take action and begin their transformational journey with you. By properly utilizing each section, they will know that you understand their problems, and have pinpointed the solution they seek. At this point, you have chosen your focus area and ideal client. Later, you can repeat the process as you expand your coaching practice.

Your messaging will be all about your ideal client, not about you.

Once you have developed your messaging you will be able to use this information in a variety of ways. For example, you can create ad copy for your marketing and package descriptions. You will also have material to use on your website and in your "About Me" sections on social media. This material will provide the foundation for your "Elevator Pitch" and how you can speak about your programs as you network.

Let's begin to work on the messaging you will create for your package or workshop using information gathered in previous exercises. As mentioned, this section is broken into six segments: Opening Statement, Challenging Questions, Knowing the Consequences, Giving Hope, Working Together, and Call to Action. Each area has a specific purpose to help you create a cohesive message to attract new clients who are ready to solve their problems.

For now, let's work specifically on the messaging you will create to sell your package or workshop.

Opening Statement

Now that you have some key words and phrases that resonate with your ideal client, let's create an opening statement that will hook your client and bring them into learning more about your services. Your opening statement has two parts: 1) it draws attention to what they are looking for, and 2) tells them what they can expect as a solution when hiring you. You want the words to create an emotional connection and move them to action to learn about working with you.

An opening statement is short, sweet and to the point. It is a lead-in sentence that draws attention to a perceived problem and promises a solution. Remember, we are working on creating messaging that allows your client to see their problems and challenges and be motivated to solve them. Here are a few examples:

> *"Improve team performance and positively impact your company's bottom line."*

> *"Coaching Managers and their teams into high-performance results."*

Launch - Creating Your Key Messaging

> *"Strategy and planning for Non-Profit Executive Directors to meet business objectives."*

> *"Bringing peace to families through improved communication."*

Use some of the key words and phrases you identified earlier and create a series of opening statements about your package or training program that your ideal client can relate to and hear. Make sure it has the two elements: the implied problem and the promised solution.

Exercise - Opening Statement

Answer the questions below. Use your Keywords and phrases and work from earlier exercises.

Who is your ideal client?

What are their challenges and problems?

What solutions are they looking for?

What solutions do you offer?

Write at least 5 Opening Statements that might resonate with your ideal client:

Challenging Questions

Questions open doors. Knowing the questions your ideal client has in their head is one of the most powerful tools that you will use to reach and engage them. Asking questions up front can get your potential client thinking about their problems. Probing questions can be used in your messaging, reminding them of their challenges and their need for a solution.

The Coach Business Guide

Whatever questions you pose, they must answer "YES!" to these questions and feel that you understand them. This will allow them to see their problems and keep them reading to see if you have answers. Here are some examples to get you started:

> "Do you lead a multigenerational team that cannot seem to communicate? Is your team dysfunctional because of misunderstandings from workers who are from different
> generations?"

> "Is your job killing you? How much more time can you afford to waste in a job that is going nowhere? Will your skills get stale because you are waiting to explore better options?"

> "Are you unhappy? Are the toxic vibes from work sucking the life out of you? Are you thoroughly exhausted when you get home from work?"

> "Are you struggling to meet your objectives? Is your turnover rate for volunteers higher than you can handle, causing stress and overwhelm for you and your people?"

The purpose of the following exercise is to help you better understand some of the most difficult questions your ideal client is trying to answer.

Launch - Creating Your Key Messaging

> ### Exercise - Challenging Questions
> In the previous exercise, you identified your ideal client's greatest challenges. Use this information, along with your answers from the Exercise - Client Transformation Journey to imagine the questions that are struggling to answer.
>
> ---
>
> *What are your ideal client's challenges and problems?*
>
> *What is keeping them up at night?*
>
> *What are some questions they are not asking because of shame or fear?*
>
> *Write several questions that you believe will cause your ideal client to make an emotional connection to their challenges.*

Knowing the Consequences

When creating a relationship with your ideal client, you need to know what the consequences are for them NOT finding a solution to their challenges. When you identify this, you can help them see the depth of their struggle and stimulate their desire to find solutions. You will use this information throughout your messaging to trigger a response from your client. This will create an emotional buy-in to finding their solutions through you.

Consider your ideal client's issues and what will happen if they fail to take action. Put them in their own story. Add supporting statements that prove your point. You want them to recognize the cost of doing nothing.

The Coach Business Guide

Here are a few examples of how you might present the consequences as a question or statement:

> *"A dysfunctional team can devastate your results and ultimately, cause miscommunication, delays, and lost revenue."*

> *"How many more conflicts do you have in your future by waiting to solve your team's communication issues?"*

> *"Don't waste your time in a job that's going nowhere. Will your skills get further behind by waiting to explore better options?"*

> *If you stay where you are you will continue to have high stress and less happiness in your job.*

> *How many more years can you stick it out?"*

> *"Where will your team be six months from now if you do nothing? Will you have another delay in your deliverables and more entrenched silos in your operation?"*

> *"Stress! Stress! Stress! It continues to pile on. The problems with your marriage are affecting you physically and mentally.*

Most people buy because they believe their purchase will result in pleasure or it will help them avoid pain. Making no decision is still a decision. Knowing the consequences of your client doing nothing is essential for you to know what you can do to help them. Understanding these negative possibilities will help you craft your message to trigger them into action.

In the next exercise, you will create your own questions or statements that speak to the consequences of doing nothing.

Launch - Creating Your Key Messaging

> ### Exercise - Knowing the Consequences
> Answer the following and create your own statements.
>
> ---
>
> *What are your ideal client's challenges and problems?*
>
> *What will get worse if they do nothing within 90 days? 6 months? 1 year?*
>
> *Write several examples that you believe will cause your ideal client to see their situation getting worse:*

Giving Hope

How do you speak about the hope you will give your clients? They need hope to see their way out of their challenging situation. By showing them that you understand the problem and the consequences, they will hear the hope you offer.

What experience will your ideal client have and what changes will they see as a result of your coaching or training? What will success look like after working with you? Paint a vision of the new reality that they may not feel is possible. Speak about how others have had success in working with you. Give them hope for the solutions you offer.

Here are a few examples of how other coaches have described this hope for their clients in their messaging. Your messaging must show your ideal client what they can expect through your coaching.

> > *"Good news: you don't have to do this alone. You can help your team connect to your company's core mission and their unique role within it. Through coaching, you will be able to see the path to gain their trust and buy in."*

> *"Others like you have found that focusing on their personal goals through coaching speeds up the process. They achieve much more because of the clarity they are able to receive with a guide by their side."*

> *"Successful managers have discovered that developing talent increases productivity by tapping into people's greatest strengths. You, too, can generate high growth by knowing what is right with your people and helping them do more of that."*

> *"Your next move could prove to be your most strategic. Powerful women like you have found themselves at the same crossroads. They found that working with an Executive Coach is beneficial in gaining clarity and mapping out next steps."*

Exercise - Giving Hope

Write your own statements to give hope. They should include the following elements: the problem your ideal client needs to solve, the solution you can provide and what others have experienced. Make sure your statements are client focused.

What changes do they want?

How does your solution solve their problem?

Launch - Creating Your Key Messaging

Working Together

Anyone interested in your coaching services will want to know how to work with you. They will be looking for your process, the value you offer, and what they can expect as an outcome.

Earlier in the book, you created your workshop or coaching package. In your planning, you determined the duration of your workshop and the number of sessions you need to achieve the objectives.

In this segment, you will be sharing a little bit about the tools, steps or processes they can expect as part of their experience with you. They begin to see that it is not just a conversation, but rather a meaningful discussion or activities they will engage in to reach their goals.

The following are examples of how some coaches describe their process and share the expected outcomes.

> *"It is easy to work together. We will customize a strategy just for you. You will soon see the results of working step-by-step through your individualized plan."*

> *"Many managers like you have found great success in my Operation Turnaround process. Together, we will go through Discovery to identify the root of the problem. Next is Solution Mapping to project outcomes. You will have guidance through the Integration, and a custom Rapid Review to show immediate signs of progress."*

> *"Your options for on-site communication training can be customized into half-day or full day experiences. Together, we will make sure every department receives the time they need so that onboarding happens company-wide in a timely manner."*

> *"You will be fully prepared to make your best career move through the Uplevel Your Career package. We will cover your unique skills and strengths, explore new possibilities and create your unique action plan through our six sessions together."*

> *"Through the 6-hour Communication Style workshop, your team will identify tactics and strategies to optimize internal communication. They will recognize their own style, and those of their peers, and know how to work together more effectively."*

Exercise - Working Together

In this exercise, answer the following questions and then describe how your ideal client will work with you.

Why is it easy to work with you?

What does your ideal client need to know about your process?

What are the key elements or steps to your package or program?

How is what you are offering aligned with your client's transformational journey?

Write several statements about how you and your ideal client will work together. Include the anticipated outcome.

Call to Action

Throughout your work as a coach, it will be necessary for you to call your ideal client to action. They might need a kick in the pants, a nudge, or a push in order for them to take the first step to work with you.

Launch - Creating Your Key Messaging

What is the next thing you want them to do? Be clear about what you are offering. You need to be comfortable inviting them to work with you. Can they opt-in to a free download of an article you have written? Schedule an appointment? Sign up for training? You have to tell them what to do. This is where many coaches offer a free 15-minute discovery call as a way to determine if there is a fit for working together. It must be clear and easy to take the next step now.

Even if you are still working on the details of your packages and services, you need to identify your ideal client's next step and make sure there is a mechanism in place for them to connect with you. Later, we offer a few suggestions if you do not have these in place yet.

Here are some examples of what other coaches have said:

> "Schedule a call with me right now by following this link to my calendar."

> "Take advantage of my free Discovery Call and let's see how we might work together."

> "Click the link now to opt-in to my free training, How to Find Your Passion!"

> "There are only two slots left for the Mastermind forming now. Click the link now and fill out your application!"

> "Click the link to learn more about the Communication Style workshop and how your team can improve productivity and performance."

> "If you are ready to Uplevel Your Career, schedule your Introductory Call now. Get started on your best career ever!"

The Coach Business Guide

Knowing what you want your ideal client to do next gives them clarity, making it easy for them to book an appointment! Be sure to know your exact process. Some examples include a free download, a link to your blog or calendar, or your phone number for them to contact you.

In the following exercise, write several phrases that call your ideal client into action. Test these with potential clients or share with your support team to see which ones get the best response.

Exercise - Call to Action
Answer the following questions to create your Call to Action phrases.

Are you offering a free introductory session? If so, how long is it, and what is it called?

Do you have a free offer or downloadable training materials?

What is the best way for a client to schedule an appointment with you?

What is the next thing you want a new prospective client to do?

Write several Call to Action phrases that guide your clients to the next step.

Pulling it All Together

Now is the time to pull together all of the information you have worked so hard on and let your potential clients see you! By creating messaging that will excite and engage your potential clients, you will gain emotional connection with your audience. Ultimately, that means more business.

Here is an example of a Career coach taking each of the ele-

Launch - Creating Your Key Messaging

ments and pulling them together into a comprehensive description of a coaching package.

Example - Pulling it All Together

Opening Statement:
Helping individuals find their next career through passion and purpose.

Challenging Questions
Is your job killing you?

Can you feel the toxic vibes when you walk in the door each morning, sucking the life out of you? How much more time can you afford to waste in a job that is going nowhere? Will your skills get further behind by waiting to explore better options?

Knowing the Consequences
If you stay where you are you will continue to have high stress and less happiness in your job. How many more years can you stick it out?"

Giving Hope
Your next move could prove to be your most strategic.

Powerful women like you have found themselves at the same crossroads. They found that working with an Executive Coach is beneficial in gaining clarity and mapping out next steps.

Working Together
Over the course of 6 weeks, you will discover your unique Superpowers, understand your best environment for advancement, and match up new career possibilities. Look forward to your next career move!

Call to Action
Take advantage of my free Discovery Call and let's see how we might work together.

Can you see how pulling this all together creates a single story line for your ideal client to follow? Do you see the advantage of breaking down the segments and putting them back together again? You have all that you need to begin creating your marketing messages!

It is your turn to take everything you have worked on so far, and create dynamic messaging that will engage your ideal client.

Exercise - Pulling it all Together

Transfer your favorite phrases from the work you have done on each of the messaging segments.

Opening Statement:

Challenging Questions:

Knowing the Consequences:

Giving Hope:

Working Together:

Call to Action:

Write your entire messaging as one description:

Did you struggle to pull it all together? Is there a segment that does not seem to fit? If you find yourself challenged, identify which area was difficult. Spend time reviewing and re-writing the different statements until they fit.

Share your final messaging with your mentor or other coaches to get their perspective. Practice speaking about your work-

Launch - Creating Your Key Messaging

shop or coaching package and the various segments to become comfortable talking about your offerings.

You have worked through the process of determining your focus area, identified your ideal client, created a workshop or coaching package and your messaging which is core to your business. You now have a way to describe what you want to do and who you will be serving.

21

Getting Your Business Started

Before you can begin coaching for income, you need to legally establish your business. There are state and federal laws that you need to adhere to, as well as tax implications that could affect your bottom line. Because these laws vary from state to state, you should consult an attorney, legal services organization or other professionals.

Take care of the legalities now so that you can begin making money and be compliant with local, state and federal laws. As with all businesses, it is important to check with your attorney or financial advisor before making any legal decisions.

Name Your Business

Naming your business does not have to be complicated. An easy solution is to use your own name as your business entity. The downside is that it is not descriptive and does not say anything about you or what you are offering. Keeping it simple is best. Your client focus may change over time. Your business name will not. As your coaching practice grows and changes, you can adapt your marketing and messaging to suit a specific product, service, or a changing market. You will want to stay consistent with your legal identity over the lifetime of your business.

We recommend brainstorming several names because your favorite may not be available in your state or as a website domain. To settle on a business name, you will need to check and confirm it is available through your state's legal authority.

Business Types

Once you have settled on the name of your business, registration is usually the next step.

Most states require you to register your coaching business with the Secretary of State's office, a Business Bureau, or a Business Agency. Research "How to start a business in ____ (your state)." You will probably find everything you need to know about starting your coaching business in your state with easy, step-by-step instructions.

Once you have done this, you will need to determine what organization type you want your business to operate under. You could establish your business as a Sole Proprietor, LLC or a Corporation, depending on your business needs and tax implications. If you are uncertain what type of entity you should set up, check with a legal or financial advisor.

You might also need to apply for a Federal Employee Identification Number (EIN). The IRS uses the EIN to identify the taxpayer. EINs are used by most businesses, regardless of business type. We all know none of us can escape death or taxes!

Do not postpone these decisions. Chances are the first package or workshop you sell is likely to put tax implications on your income. Professional coaches adhere to all applicable laws and guidelines. Check local laws, a legal services organization, or

Launch - Getting Your Business Started

a financial advisor to help you determine your next steps and any annual reporting requirements.

Getting Paid

In today's rapidly evolving technology environment, you need to have multiple options available so you can be paid. Corporations may still pay you the old-fashioned way, through a check or direct deposit. Individuals might want credit card options, payment service or digital wallet.

Managing the money in your business is not something to be taken lightly. This is when you might need financial, legal and tax advice.

You will need to think about money in three ways:
- How you send a bill/invoice
- How someone pays you
- How you track your money

In order to launch your business, you may not need a payment system at all. A simple way could be to create an invoice, have your client send a check by mail, and manually track revenue and expenses. At minimum, you need a separate checking account for your business to track expenses and income. There are tax implications and other legalities around commingling money between your personal and business life. Check with your financial or legal advisor.

In the next exercise, you will determine how you will get paid, and how you will track your money from your coaching practice.

In the next exercise, you will determine how you will get paid, and how you will track your money from your coaching practice.

Exercise - Getting Paid
Answer the following to make sure you are ready to get paid.

Have you opened a bank account in your business name?

How will you send invoices?

Will you require payment in full? Will you offer payment options?

Will you accept credit cards? If so, how?

Will you accept money from a payment service and/or digital wallet service?

How will you track income and expenses?

Did you find any areas that require your attention? Were there any questions that you were unable to answer? Have you identified a financial or legal advisor?

The demographics of your clients and the type of coaching business you want to have will guide you in determining which financial tools you will need. Do your research and choose the financial tools that offer features that will keep your business organized and legal.

22

Getting Your First Clients

In this section, you have completed a lot of work with respect to your messaging, your business set-up, and how you plan to get paid. There are just a few more things you need to spend time working on in order to successfully launch your practice.

These include:

- Scheduling
- Virtual Coaching
- Basic Online Presence
- Other Messaging Needs

Many coaches believe they need a full-blown website in order to launch their business. This can be an expensive and time-consuming process. Consider instead, a simple landing page or profile page where your ideal client can discover information about your services, your packages and book an appointment.

Scheduling

How are your clients going to schedule their appointments with you? You may start out making appointments manually with a paper calendar. This will soon become cumbersome, and your clients may see you as less than professional. You want to make it easy for your clients to pick times that are convenient for them, and that fit your schedule without having to go through you directly.

Automation is your friend when it comes to your calendar. There are free calendar systems that you can start with and move into a paid version when you are ready. Find the tool that is easy to use, fits your needs and your current technology.

Here are some questions to ask when choosing a scheduling platform:

- Is it mobile friendly?
- Is it easy to set up?
- Can your client book/cancel their appointments?
- Does it send reminders?
- Can it be integrated with your current technology and email management programs?
- Does it have search capabilities?
- Can you communicate with your clients through the platform?
- How long has the platform existed?
- Does the technology support how your services are delivered?
- Do you get a trial period to test it to confirm it meets your needs?
- Is a long-term contract required?

Whichever scheduling system you choose, open an account and look at additional features they provide that you might upgrade to in the future. Be careful going with a free service that will not be able to support your future needs.

Launch - Getting Your First Clients

Virtual Coaching

The world of coaching has dramatically changed over the past few years. Today, most clients demand virtual coaching for themselves and their employees. It is convenient, efficient, and provides flexibility.

You can provide virtual coaching through the phone or one of the many video platforms available. Technology is constantly changing and there are new options coming out with greater security and functionality, as well as additional tools and resources. Regardless of the tool you use, your clients expect their conversations to be confidential and private.

Ask these questions when choosing a technology platform:

- Is it safe and secure?
- Is it mobile friendly?
- Is there a screen share option?
- Can you host multiple people in a group call?
- What are the capacity limits for participants?
- What are the time limitations for calls?
- Can you record sessions and share them with your clients?
- Is your Wifi strong enough to handle the platform you have chosen?

Choose the platform that will allow you to launch your business today and set up an account. Practice using the tool before your first coaching session! Make sure you have a space where you can hold confidential coaching sessions.

Basic Online Presence

Developing your basic online profile helps your prospective clients learn about you and what you offer. As you start out, most new clients will likely come through referrals. People who know you, like you and trust you will be the first ones to recommend you. How and where are their referrals going to find information about you and your services?

You need a place to be seen and heard. Consider a simple landing or profile page where potential clients can discover more about your services, your packages, and book an appointment. Start with where your ideal client can be found, as these are often the first places where they will have an opportunity to discover you. By building a basic online profile you will be able to post your information on multiple platforms.

Most coaches write a paragraph telling about themselves, their certifications, their education, their job history, and blah, blah, blah.... Your potential clients do not care about your credentials until they know you care about their problem and stand ready with solutions.

Your profile is like real estate. You are hanging out your shingle and there is a door that people need to walk through in order to work with you. Is that door open or closed? If you make this space all about you, then your ideal client never makes an emotional connection. We suggest an engaging way of presenting yourself that is highly focused on your prospective client's challenges and the solutions you can provide. Your clients are looking for solutions first, then will look more closely at your experience and credentials.

You will use the coaching package or workshop description you created earlier. By adding a link to your scheduling system and short biography, your potential client sees exactly what they are searching for and can easily book an appointment.

Short Biography

Once you have shown your prospective client that you understand their problem and have a solution, it is entirely appropriate to add a few simple sentences that hold the essence of who you are, your skills, credentials and expertise. These are

Launch - Getting Your First Clients

secondary until you have made an emotional connection. It is only in support of their decision that they will want to know more about you.

Many coaches have invested in obtaining numerous certifications and are highly educated. We want to caution you about using industry specific or internal language, as it can be confusing. In your short biography, you want to be clear and concise and limit the information to that which highlights your capabilities and is relevant to your solutions.

You will want to write this personal information in the third person and can include the following:

- Your name
- Your company name (if you have one)
- Your focus
- Relevant work experience, skills and expertise
- Relevant certifications and achievements

Here are examples of what we mean by being clear and concise and avoiding a lot of industry or internal language. Sometimes, clients are looking for a specific certification or experience.

> *Amy Smith started her consulting company, A Better Future, five years ago with a desire to help women identify new career opportunities. Her 17 years in human resources in the automobile industry provides the experience needed to craft a path of advancement. Master Coach and member of National Career Development Association.*

> *Bob Smith is the founder of Fitness for Life, a wellness company specializing in creating healthy lifestyles for men over 50 looking to reclaim the vibrancy of their youth. As a fitness instructor with a focus on nutrition, his 25 years experience enables him to craft individualized plans for each client. Bob is recognized as a Top Ten Instructor for the state of Maryland and is certified in Senior Fitness.*

> *John Doe started Strengths Performance Accelerator to work with mid-sized companies improving sales team performance by focusing on strengths-based development. His 25 years' experience as a top performing sales executive, coupled with his Gallup Strengths Coaching certification, enables him to create customized workshops that drive increased sales.*

In the next exercise, you will be crafting your own short biography.

Exercise: Short Biography

Exercise: Short Biography
Using your name, company name, focus, relevant work experience, skills, expertise, certification and achievements, write your short biography in 2-5 sentences.

You have already completed the foundation for your basic online presence in the *Exercise - Pulling it All Together*. Here is the example we used earlier, describing a 6-week One-to-One coaching package aimed at a professional woman in the automobile industry. You will note that we changed our Call to Action slightly by adding a link to schedule an appointment, as well as a short biography.

Launch - Getting Your First Clients

> ### Example - "About" Section on Social Media
>
> *Helping individuals find their next career through passion and purpose.*
>
> *Is your job killing you? Can you feel the toxic vibes when you walk in the door each morning, sucking the life out of you? How much more time can you afford to waste in a job that is going nowhere? Will your skills get further behind by waiting to explore better options?*
>
> *If you stay where you are you will continue to have more stress and less happiness in your job. How many more years can you stick it out?" Your next move could prove to be your most strategic. Powerful women like you have found themselves at the same crossroads. They found that working with an Executive Coach is beneficial in gaining clarity and mapping out next steps.*
>
> *Over the course of 6 weeks, you will discover your unique Superpowers, understand your best environment for advancement, and match up new career possibilities. Look forward to your next career move!*
>
> *Take advantage of my free Discovery Call and let's see how we might work together. Follow the link to my scheduler: www.YourSchedulingSystemLink.com.*
>
> ### Short Biography:
> *Amy Smith started her consulting company, A Better Future, five years ago with a desire to help women identify new career opportunities. Her 17 years in human resources in the automobile industry provides the experience needed to craft a path of advancement. Master Coach and member of National Career Development Association.*

As you can see, your basic online presence speaks directly to your client first. Remember, even though the field on your computer screen might imply that you are to write about yourself, we want you to talk directly to your prospects instead.

Create your own description, adding in your scheduling link and short biography and you are ready to use it on various social media and other business profiles. Your clients can now find you, get information about what you offer, and book an appointment.

You are Launched!

Congratulations! You have completed all of the work necessary to get your first clients!

This is an exciting milestone for you in creating and launching your coaching business! It is time to celebrate all the work you have done! You have enough information about your offerings to share with your closest influencers and begin building your network.

Now, let's change your focus. It's time to work on growing your coaching business.

Grow

>
> *Only those who will risk going too far can possibly find out how far one can go.*
>
> - T.S. Elliott

23

Growing Your Business

Now that your coaching practice is established and launched, it is time to grow. Unfortunately, your clients will not just appear out of nowhere because you hang out your shingle. It takes discipline, planning and work to generate a full pipeline of potential clients who need your help.

This section is full of ways for you to develop a thriving coaching business now that the fundamentals are in place. We will be referencing your previous work in this section, expanding upon your ideas and integrating them into your marketing.

Marketing Yourself

One of the most difficult challenges to overcome as a coach is learning how to market yourself. It can feel icky and uncomfortable. You have probably been taught not to "toot your own horn", yet that is exactly what you must do. Marketing yourself can be done in a multitude of ways, and by attempting different strategies, you will soon identify the ones that feel right and generate the leads you need to grow your practice.

Experiment! Be okay with failing, knowing that you have at least learned what does not work! Then, try something else. Many coaches fail to market themselves, and because of that their practice fails. They do not do enough "trial and error" in order to get it right. Keep this in mind as you attempt new strategies and know that you really are moving forward.

24

Referrals and Testimonials

You will likely have people who know you, like you, and trust you enough to hire you without a lot of selling. Nurture those relationships and reach out to them about your new business. These people are your greatest source of new business referrals. Ask your current clients if they know anyone who could use your services and if they are willing to pass on your information. Use your messaging to describe your ideal client to help them identify potential prospects for what you offer.

There are many ways for you to ask for referrals. Make it easy for people to recommend you by sending a link to share with others. Add a link to the bottom of a Thank You email inviting them to tell people who would benefit from your services. Develop a reward program and offer something of value -- perhaps an extra coaching session -- to those who refer new clients.

Your clients are also your best source of testimonials. We live in a society today where people do their research before they hire a coach. They will want to access testimonials to learn about you and how others have experienced your services. Testimonials can be used in many marketing strategies and are especially important for your social media visibility.

The best time to ask for a testimonial or referral is immediately after you have helped your client reach a goal or achieve something. You can make it easy by sending an email with a link for them to write their testimonial. Sometimes, your client will even invite you to write it for them. Take advantage of that and draft one for their approval!

In the following exercise, you will identify those who can refer you now, who can provide testimonials, and how you will engage with them.

Exercise - Referrals and Testimonials
Answer the following to uncover possible referrals and testimonials.

Name five people who will provide you with a referral and/or testimonial.

How will you ask them for a referral?

What is your preferred manner of introduction to a new potential client?

Will you offer a reward for referrals?

Where will you direct them to share their review or testimonial?

Were you able to identify at least five people who will refer you to others or offer you a testimonial? Do you see why having a basic online presence helps people to access your information? Adding testimonials will help reinforce the services you provide and endorse you as a professional. When you receive referrals or testimonials, be sure to follow up immediately with a thank you email or a phone call.

25

Networking

New clients can be found in a variety of places. The challenge is to identify a few groups, organizations, events and activities where you can find them. Every communication you have or event you attend is a potential opportunity. Show up professionally, be ready to meet people and discover new circles of influence.

If you are uncomfortable networking, you can attend events with people you know. Working together, you can bolster each other's confidence and be there for moral support. You will discover additional tactics with each new event you attend. In time, you will identify your comfort zone.

Networking Opportunities

There are many places where you can network informally, especially where you routinely go as part of your everyday life. Consider what is available in your local community such as your church or synagogue, the school where your kids attend, a party in the neighborhood, your HOA meeting, your fitness center, or the bank, to name a few.

There are numerous formal networking organizations where you can find prospective clients and build referral relationships. Some are free, others are pay-to-play and can be costly. A local chapter of a business networking organization or local community group like a Chamber of Commerce might be options. You can also search relevant professional organizations, alumni groups, conferences, and community service clubs among others. Perhaps becoming a board member for your favorite non-profit is the perfect place for you to meet new people.

Online Networking is a popular way to meet new people and build your visibility. Some organizations are now scheduling online networking events, allowing participants to share information about the services they provide and the people they are looking to serve. Participating in chat rooms or groups where your clients can be found is another way to network.

New clients can come from a variety of formal and informal networking efforts. The secret is finding a match between what you are comfortable doing and where your ideal prospects can be found.

Use the next exercise to identify your formal and informal networking opportunities.

Grow - Networking

> ## Exercise - Networking Opportunities
> Answer the following to identify networking opportunities.
>
> ---
>
> *Write down five places where they may be found.*
>
> *What places do you visit each week where you might encounter them?*
>
> *What are the professional networking groups in your area?*
>
> *What organizations or community service clubs are you interested in where they might be found?*
>
> *What alumni or social groups do you have access to that are relevant?*
>
> *What conferences can you attend where you will encounter them?*
>
> *What online platform chat rooms or groups can you participate in and contribute where they can be found?*
>
> *What are two networking opportunities or events that you will commit to attend within the next 30 days?*

Were you able to identify at least five networking opportunities? Did you expand your thinking about where you can find your ideal client?

A big mistake coaches make is attending a lot of events without a good strategy. They do not know where their potential clients will be, or at which events they may encounter them. Be selective and attend those networking events where you are likely to get the best results.

Preparing to Network

If you are out and about in your community, you should always be prepared to meet new people. Networking can happen at any time and any place. You need to be ready to talk about your coaching business and the services you provide to anyone you meet.

Preparing for a networking event requires some planning. This can give you an edge and increase your confidence.

If possible, review the guest list and do your research on the actual event and likely attendees. Identify who you want to meet and set a clear objective. Reach out in advance and let them know you would like to meet them. Or, find someone in your network who might know them and can facilitate an introduction.

Before the event make sure you have identified a way to share your business information such as business cards. Spend time preparing what you will say when you introduce yourself and how you will respond to questions. Plan how you will capture information about the people you meet to ensure meaningful follow up.

You can do this! You are the best person to represent your new company!

What do you do?

As you are networking, "What do you do?" is the question that you must be able to answer in a way that is natural, confident, and conversational. Include enough information to let the listener know what kind of coaching practice you have and the services you provide. It is usually inappropriate to sell when you are networking. Networking is merely a way for you to expand the number of people you know who might lead you to new business.

Grow - Networking

Look back at the *Exercise - Pulling it All Together* where you completed your workshop or package description. Use this material to create your own introduction. This is easy and can be adapted according to your audience. You will use this to answer the question, "What do you do?"

The following exercise will help you get prepared for any networking event.

Exercise - What Do You Do?

Answer the following questions with the response you would make at a networking event.

Tell me more about how you work?

What is coaching? How is it different from therapy?

What makes your coaching unique?

How long have you been in business?

Is this your full-time job?

Do you offer virtual coaching?

Do you target a particular industry?

Do you have a certain client you work with most?

What do you look for in a company that you might want to work with?

Who do you want to be connected to?

How can I help you?

Not everyone is comfortable networking, yet it is a critical activity to find new clients. You need to build confidence being around strangers, meeting new people, and proactively introducing yourself. Be prepared to answer some basic questions and have questions of your own to ask. This will bring confidence and build your professional network. Practice with friends and family who know you, like you and trust you, and who will give you honest feedback.

What Do You Do in Reverse

When networking, you are talking about yourself, but you want to learn as much as possible about the other person and their business. Using our earlier example of a career coach working in the automobile industry, we are showing ways to introduce yourself and begin a networking conversation.

> *"My name is Amy Smith, and I am a career coach. I work with those who are looking for passion and purpose in their next career move. What do you do?"*

> *"My name is Amy Smith, and I am a career coach who works with people whose job is killing them. We work together to identify their passions and purpose, and ultimately, their next career move to get them out of a toxic environment. What do you do?"*

> *"I am Amy Smith, and I work with women in the automobile industry. I help them with their next career move by identifying their passion and purpose with my Uplevel Your Career coaching program. What do you do?"*

Grow - Networking

> *"I am Amy Smith, and I am looking for women in the automobile industry who are in a toxic environment and are looking to get out and into their next career. What do you do?"*

> *"I am Amy Smith, and I offer a great, 6-week coaching program for women who are looking to get out of a toxic work environment and into a new career opportunity. What do you do?"*

Notice that we added "What do you do?" after the introduction, putting the focus back on them! Here is the secret: the person asking the most questions maintains control of the conversation. By asking questions, you are showing an interest in them.

Here are some sample questions that go beyond "What do you do?":

- Why are you here?
- Have you been to this event before?
- How do you use these networking events?
- What kind of clients are you looking for?
- Who can I connect you to?
- What is your biggest challenge right now?
- How can I help you?

The key to success is to learn as much about the other people who are at the event. Networking is reciprocal. It is not just about you hunting for new clients. Networking is also about finding ways that you can help others. By making connections for those in your networking circles, they will naturally look for ways to reciprocate and help you.

Ultimately, the questions may come back to you and what you do. You will want to be prepared with descriptions to speak about your coaching, who you help and the outcomes of working with you in a general way.

Networking Objectives

One thing many coaches do when attending a networking event is to "canvas the crowd" and meet as many people as possible. This is a mistake. Instead, set an objective to meet two or three people with whom you will have a conversation about your coaching practice. This is more effective than handing out twenty business cards to random people.

Another goal is to discover where you can give referrals. The Law of Reciprocity says that what you give, you get. Finding business for other people will spark in them the desire to find business and make introductions on your behalf. Networking is all about connecting and having meaningful conversations, even if only for a few minutes.

Networking Follow Up

The fortune is in the follow up!

Many coaches feel that when they leave a networking event, they are finished. In reality, you have to continue to work that event through your follow up activities. Connecting formally through social media, sending a follow up email or reaching out to connect for coffee needs to be done immediately, within 48 hours. The truth is, as time passes, they may not remember you and you may have lost any potential opportunities.

Current studies show that it takes 5-7 attempts to communicate with and capture a new client. Your follow up should include a reminder of who you are, what you do, and some form of help. You could share an article, a tip or an idea that is relevant. By providing something of value in your communication, you show that you want to serve them. When you help someone with no strings attached, there will be a natural desire to return the favor.

We cannot stress enough how important it is to follow up.

26

Developing Your Brand

In this chapter, we break down the details of how to become recognized for what you bring to the marketplace. So far, you have built the basics of your "brand" through the work you have done on your messaging. Let's expand that and bring in other aspects of your brand.

What is your brand? Some coaches think that their logo is their brand, but it is so much more than that. Your business brand encompasses the visual and written representation of who you are and what your business stands for. When your ideal client sees or reads something about you or your coaching practice, it must resonate with them.

You have worked on your messaging and have used it to create your coaching package or workshop description and your basic online presence. Let's focus on the visual representation of your coaching practice.

Brand Imagery

How do you want to be seen in the marketplace? Your brand imagery is how you are viewed in public when you are not present. Anything that your ideal client can see about you in the marketplace needs to create an emotional connection. By having the right imagery and complementing colors, you can instill a positive reaction about you and your services.

As you build your image, you will need to choose pictures for your website, packages, social media and other marketing collateral. You will also need to choose a color palette that reflects your personality, style and business.

In the following exercise, you will do some research on your visuals and color palette. Look at competitors' websites and other sites where your ideal client may be searching for information. For example, if you are a Health and Wellness coach, search keywords like "fitness," "healthy lifestyle," or "wellness," and look through free image files online. Check our website at www.CoachBusinessGuide.com for more information.

Exercise - Brand Imagery

Refer to previous exercises to complete the following in your journal.

What keywords and phrases have you selected?

What is your focus area?

What images immediately come to mind when thinking about your ideal client?

What visuals do you see on competitor websites?

Search online for photos on free photo apps and select those that are in alignment with your coaching practice.

Use an online color palette generator to find color combinations that you like. Choose a few that resonate with both you and your ideal client.

Grow - Developing Your Brand

As you move further into developing your marketing materials, your brand imagery needs to fit not only who you are, but how your prospective clients will react when seeing it. Have you identified the visuals that speak to the solutions they are looking for?

Now that you have an idea of what visuals align with you, your ideal client and your messaging, you will be able to use this information when working with web and graphic designers.

Logo Development

If you are just starting out, our very best advice is to not get caught up in designing the perfect logo. You can use an online service to create your own or hire an inexpensive design service. Many coaches simply choose a fancy font script, especially if they operate their business under their personal name.

If you do decide to create a logo, here are some tips:

- Make it easy to read
- Ensure it can work in black and white as well as color
- Make sure it can fit in a small space
- Allow room for your tagline, if applicable
- Create different versions, such as .jpg, .png, .pdf

Many coaches begin without a logo. When you become a large corporation and go through a rebrand, then you can invest a small fortune in your new logo! Over time you may decide it is appropriate to create one. Thinking about these things in advance will prepare you to work with a designer later on.

27

Marketing Assets

Marketing assets are the tools you use to build your brand and share information about your practice, events and training. These materials need to represent you and the value of the solutions your coaching brings to a client. Marketing assets can be print material or digital media. Your logo, brand image, color palette, and messaging all need to be complementary.

Think carefully about your needs before you go out and create a lot of different marketing assets. Your highest objective right now is income producing activity. As long as a prospective client knows how to reach you and book an appointment, you are good to go. Limit the creation of your marketing assets to only those items you need immediately. You will develop additional items over time. Let's start with some basics.

Print and Promotional Collateral

Print collateral refers to anything that promotes your business and is on paper, like business cards, brochures, and announcements that you hand out during networking and other occasions. These are inexpensive and can be easily developed with online tools. By creating print materials, you will be prepared when you are out in the marketplace. We recommend including a photo of yourself, your contact information and logo, if applicable. If you are using a business card, take advantage of the backside and use this space to include a tagline, a link to your digital training, or a favorite quote.

As the need arises, you can create flyers, brochures or other print collateral to provide information about a workshop or a future event. These can provide details about the training and coaching that you offer and can give a deeper insight into your business. Use these materials for mail distribution, to hand out during presentations and at networking events.

Promotional items are things like coffee mugs, magnets, pens, hand sanitizer, etc. A pen, for example, can be used to open the door to additional conversations. Think ahead to the next conference or event where you might sponsor a table or booth. These goodies are excellent giveaways if they have your logo or contact information printed on them.

The following exercise will allow you to take stock of what promotional items you already have and determine what you may need in the immediate future.

Exercise - Promotional Assets and Needs

Answer the following to assess your print and promotional needs.

What promotional items do you already have? Include logo, business cards, workshop fliers, brochures or other items you have already created. List the item and topic.

Where will you be distributing them?

List the promotional items you need to have created.

Who will create these items?

What is your budget for print and promotional assets?

Create - Marketing Assets

When you identified your short-term promotional needs, were you able to determine how you will use them? If not, you may not need them. We want to reiterate - focus on your immediate needs. Do not try to create everything at once. When you are starting your coaching practice, talking to people about what you do and who you serve is more effective than handing out a brochure.

Digital Marketing Assets

Marketing assets can often be converted to a digital format and used online as well as in print. For example, a research paper you have developed could be converted to .pdf and sent online in an email or be printed and handed out personally. A brochure can be posted online or used at a networking event as a printed invitation. You can also create a digital business card and signature.

Memes, articles, quotes, infographics and videos are also digital assets. This is content that you post across your social media platforms to engage with your clients. You can repurpose this content by incorporating it into your brochures, flyers and email marketing. Be aware of copyright laws if you are referencing someone's copyrighted material.

If you are making an offer to opt-in to a free resource or you are selling a workshop or coaching package, an easy option is to have a landing page. A landing page can work without a website and is a way to get started without investing the time and money to build one. Your social media platforms can be used to share information until you are ready.

28

Developing Marketing Content

One of the biggest challenges for coaches is finding and creating enough content to consistently engage their audience. Your content must always be fresh and current. It takes time and planning to keep abreast of trends. Having a pool of resources where you can get ideas for new content and material will make your life easier.

Here are different types of marketing content you might find helpful:

Articles - You can write your own or share articles authored by someone who has a similar philosophy or who shares your views. Search keywords on the internet that include your favorite topics and complement your coaching style and areas of focus. Subscribe to blogs of favorite authors that also support your calling, vision and beliefs and share their content with your audience. Do not be afraid to share information from other sources. You are doing a service to your clients by offering them different points of view around the same topics.

Quotes - Quotes are an easy way to quickly populate your social platforms with relevant messages that complement your own. You can fill in gaps in your marketing with quick, inspirational messages that keep people engaged. There are many quote websites available on the internet and using your keywords, you can find dozens that relate to your program offerings. There are also simple graphic programs available where you can create imagery that is aligned with your brand.

Memes - Memes are a popular way to spread your messaging through imagery. A meme is an image or a GIF video, that may or may not contain words. It represents the thoughts or feelings of a specific audience. The memes you post need to be interesting to your ideal client. They can teach principles very quickly, usually in a humorous way. You can repeat them often to get your message across.

Infographics - An infographic uses imagery, charts, data and minimal text to quickly convey a concept. They usually contain more information than a meme and tell a complete story about a specific idea or principle. There are online programs that can help you build an infographic quickly, or you can outsource this to professionals.

Videos - Creating videos of yourself teaching a concept, sharing an inspiring word, or other short broadcasts can be used to market yourself and your business. Shorter recordings are always better. Giving your potential clients an experience of you and your style will encourage them to engage with you. As they watch and learn from your videos, they will take advantage of opting-in to get additional information about you. Your videos should always include a Call to Action, like an invitation to make an appointment.

These are just a few examples of the different types of content that you can use. Be aware of getting caught up in creating too many different items. Avoid plagiarism by always giving credit or citation to all third-party information and quotes. You can outsource the creation of your memes and infographic design to a professional. Remember, your job is to coach, not be a graphic designer!

Grow - Developing Marketing Content

The next exercise will allow you to identify the marketing content you have right now and discover what you need in order to fully engage with your ideal client.

Exercise - Marketing Content
Answer the following to determine your marketing content.

What marketing content do you have in the form of blog posts, articles, memes, or other items you have already created?

What materials do you need to create or acquire to help support your clients?

List five topics for articles that will educate and attract.

List ten quotes you can use to inspire.

List five meme topics that will effectively engage.

List data or facts that will be of interest.

List five topics for short videos that train or educate.

What websites will you be able to search for relevant content?

Who will help you create this content?

Who will schedule this content on your social channels?

Were you able to identify topics and information of interest to your ideal client? Do you see how this provides the material you can use to create your content? Now, it is just a matter of gathering that content and scheduling it. Be sure to cite any copyrighted material. Once your content and materials have been created, you will be able to place it on various social media sites.

29

Social Media

In order to be successful, you must use and engage on multiple social media platforms. There are many of them available today and the challenge is to identify where your prospects are likely to be found.

Once you know where your ideal client is active, those are the platforms you need to focus on. Learn and master how to interact with your clients where they are. It is very easy to get caught up in wanting to be everywhere. We recommend you participate on just a few sites to get the value of your time investment.

Once you have identified which platforms you will use, then develop a strategy and set goals to share your marketing content. Take the time to research how other coaches may be using these platforms. After you have determined your strategy and gathered your material, you will be able to outsource it to a virtual assistant or maybe even a teenager you trust!

Social Media Posting Calendar

Creating a social media posting calendar is one way to organize the materials you will use across all your channels. It allows you to plan a consistent posting schedule.

You can easily create your schedule by downloading a blank calendar for each of your social media channels and fill in what you are going to post and when. This will give you an idea of what you need to find or create to share. You already created a foundation for this in the *Exercise - Marketing Content.*

Remember, you can repurpose the same content across multiple platforms and repeat them periodically. Once your calendar is complete, you can outsource this to a virtual assistant and have your content posted without you even being involved! There are also tools that will allow you to schedule your postings a month or more in advance.

30

Public Speaking and Events

Public speaking is a great way to showcase your talents, your expertise and improve your name brand recognition. Once you have identified your presentation topics, you can then create multiple presentations to fill any length of time requested. The key is to deliver relevant content that is useful, allows the audience to have an experience of your style and the value your services bring to the market.

The speeches you give must be in alignment with your messaging. The simplest way to develop this type of content is to pull from your broader materials. Be as generous as possible with your content. Feel free to give as much away as you are comfortable with, because your clients cannot implement or utilize your content without you.

Look for opportunities to speak at community organizations like the Rotary, the Chamber of Commerce or local conferences. Churches, social clubs, and alumni associations often look for guest speakers, as well. All of these are opportunities for you to share your knowledge and expertise. Often, a small crowd provides the perfect intimacy to deeply engage with your clients.

Here are a few questions to ask in order to qualify an opportunity before saying, "Yes!" to any speaking engagement:

- Does the audience represent your ideal client?
- Is the topic requested in alignment with your messaging?
- Will you have access to the registration details, so that you can do your own follow up?
- Can you hand out your marketing material and contact information?
- Are you able to make an offer of your services to the audience?
- Do you see any potential future business opportunities by speaking at this event?
- Does the environment offer everything you need to speak effectively?
- Are you able to have access to a recording to use in your marketing?

Speaking in front of any size audience is the perfect opportunity for your prospective clients to see you in action. Finding or hiring someone who can take pictures or record your presentation can provide you additional content that you can use on your website or in social posts. These become valuable marketing assets that you will use over and over.

Remember, any speech you develop can always be repurposed. You can use it to create blog posts, white papers or even an eBook!

31

Multiple Streams of Income

As your business grows, you will start to identify many new opportunities for you to expand your coaching practice and diversify your revenue. This will give you enough variety to protect you in the event that a contract ends. If you are an independent contractor coaching or training within an organization, you are always at the mercy of someone else's budget. Identifying new income streams can protect you when decisions are made that are out of your control.

There are a lot of ways you can diversify. Here are a few ideas:

- Turn your in person workshop into an online training program
- Create a workshop from a speech
- Become an adjunct professor at a local community college
- Be a mentor coach for a certification program
- Partner with another coach and create a joint venture
- Earn affiliate revenue by referring products and tools of the industry
- Write a book

Too many coaches end up in a "feast or famine" situation, especially during the holidays and other "dry spells." Generating income in a variety of ways will ensure the financial stability of your coaching practice.

Continue to Grow

As you have now learned, a lot is involved in order to grow and sustain a vibrant coaching business. Your success is dependent upon how well you develop your brand and become known for who you work with and the services you provide. Being able to succinctly and clearly describe your coaching practice will allow you to gain additional referrals and build your networking relationships.

Most coaches go through this process multiple times as they change and grow and as their clientele expands. Make a calendar entry to revisit your messaging, marketing materials and networking strategies at least every quarter. This will ensure that your coaching practice stays fresh.

32

Tools for Continued Growth

Your new coaching business will grow and evolve in ways that you may not be able to see right now. In this section, we provide additional information that will support your coaching efforts and help you successfully manage and operate your business. Having the right tools adds to your credibility and professionalism. We are not providing specific platforms or links because technology changes so quickly.

Certifications and Professional Organizations

Depending upon your unique coaching focus, a coaching certification may give you the credentials that you need. A certification is not important to some clients, while for others, it is a requirement.

Coaches can obtain certifications from a variety of sources. Choose wisely. Pick an organization that provides the best in-depth material, knowledge base and continuing education so that you can be constantly improving your coaching skills. Consider your ideal client when selecting a certification program.

Many professional coaching organizations will provide certifications, group resources, discounts, and continuing education. Think through the value and return you will get before investing in any certification.

Contracts

Coaches need basic contracts in order to operate and protect themselves. One way to ensure commitment to your program and create dependable income is to develop a coaching agreement (or contract) for your clients. These will be determined by how you work, the services you are providing, and who you are serving. This is especially true if you are working with businesses and organizations. Laying out the terms of your services will provide clarity and set expectations.

You may offer customized packages or training programs that need to be protected by copyright or trademark because they are your unique intellectual property. Depending on your clients and your focus area, you might need a non-disclosure agreement. If you develop a joint venture with another coach, an operating agreement will lay out the details for income and expenses. Government contract work will likely require registration and other documents depending on the work being provided.

Work with an attorney or legal membership service to create templates for your most commonly used contracts.

Legal and Insurance Services

Your business needs more than a bank account and registration with your state (refer to the Chapter - Getting Your Business Started). If you were sued, who would you call? There are legal membership services that will allow you to access credible legal advice and guidance at a group rate.

Some of the organizations you will work with may require you to have professional liability insurance. There are numerous carriers that provide commercial insurance at a reasonable price. Check with your personal insurance company for recommendations.

Research membership programs that combine the buying power of their members to get the best price for legal and insurance services.

Customer Relationship Management (CRM)

As we have said before, the fortune is in the follow up. Many coaches get busy and forget to keep in touch with past clients or nurture current prospects. You either nurture your clients, or they will forget you and hire the next coach that comes along. You can start with a spreadsheet, but as your business grows, investing in a Customer Relationship Management (CRM) system will make you efficient. With a CRM, you can set up a monthly newsletter or schedule relevant and timely content to be distributed to your entire email list.

Again, be sure to follow up within 48 hours of meeting a new connection or attending a networking event. Create templates to manage your communication so you can enter contact information and send quickly. You will keep your new relationship moving forward by reaching out immediately. Top of mind awareness is invaluable.

Learning Management System (LMS)

A Learning Management System (LMS) is a platform that enables you to upload your recorded digital content and training materials which can be accessed by anyone at any time. This provides an opportunity to scale your business by doing the work once, uploading it to an LMS and selling it, giving access over and over again.

This is not for the faint of heart! You must develop the content, record the training, create the worksheets, and then upload everything to the LMS platform. The greatest benefit is that you are doing the work once and creating an "evergreen" product that you can promote as part of your coaching practice. You can save time by recording your live trainings and uploading them to your LMS.

When you are ready to start, there are numerous systems to choose from. Determining your best options will depend on your budget, your ideal client, and your skill level.

Text Messaging Platforms

In addition to email, text messaging is an effective way to deliver links and engage your audience. Studies show that email open rates are between 15-25%, while open rates of text messages are up to 98%! Observe your own behavior: how many texts do you open vs. email?

Texting can even become a component of your coaching services by allowing you to respond to your clients quickly. Studies suggest that responding within five minutes of an inquiry can significantly increase your close rate. You can offer text reminders for upcoming appointments, as well as encouragement and check-ins. Giving your clients access to you during the course of your coaching packages can keep them engaged and moving forward. Make sure your client can opt-in and opt-out just as quickly.

Video

Today, video content is highly popular for most consumers and getting your message out through video must be part of your overall marketing strategy. You can add video content by live streaming or by uploading recordings. Some social media platforms give live video a higher priority than uploaded video.

It takes guts to go live, where every wrinkle shows, every mis-

Grow - Tools for Continued Growth

take is seen, and you sometimes just make it up as you go. As you grow in experience, you will start to get a handle on what your audience really wants. Soon, a structure will form organically and it will get easier. You can start by using your cell phone, or your virtual coaching platform tools. Plan several shows out before you begin so that you feel prepared and confident.

Keep Growing!

The coaching industry continues to change and grow as new trends arise. You will change and grow as well. Don't be afraid to experiment and explore new opportunities, as this is the path for growth. Sometimes you will fail. Learn from that and move on!

Check our website at www.CoachBusinessGuide.com for more information, resources and strategies to keep growing your coaching business.

Final Thoughts of the Book

As we wrap up your journey along the path to launch and grow your coaching practice, we want you to prepare for one thing - *change*. You will constantly be evolving your skills and experience and adding to your credentials throughout your coaching journey. Where you are today is lightyears away from where you will be two years from now! By continually looking at what you are doing, being open to change and trying new things, your coaching practice will take off and bloom! Many coaches struggle with making changes and testing the outcomes to increase their revenue and client base. Make sure you have a support team you can call upon to hold you accountable and provide help.

If you find at any point that things become stagnant or your business is not growing, come back and work through this material again. Consider who you are serving now and what is different. What materials or new programs can you add to your list of services that will attract new clients and expand your business?

Your priority should be to reinvest in your business by improving your programs and expanding your marketing efforts before seeking additional certifications. It is easy to get frustrated on this journey of launching and growing your coaching business. Keep in mind that flexibility is your friend. It will take time before seeing the full return of your efforts.

You have everything you need to launch an amazing coaching practice! We wish you great success in your new coaching career!

We look forward to hearing from you! You can find us at: www.CoachBusinessGuide.com

Anne and Rhonda

About the Authors

Rhonda Knight Boyle is a transformational leader and Gallup-Certified Strengths Coach. She's the best selling author of Turning Talents into Strengths: Stories of Coaching Transformation and host of the CoachTalk TV show on YouTube. Rhonda has been part of the strengths movement since 2008 and is also a Certified Law of Attraction facilitator with a special emphasis on Neuroscience principles.

Anne Herbster is a marketing and sales executive with more than 30 years in nonprofit and Fortune 100 companies. Her extensive background includes working with startup companies building face-to-face and online coaching programs and driving revenue. She brings a strong passion in focusing on the optimum customer experience that drives retention. Anne graduated with an MBA in finance and marketing from Columbia University.